HUMANS

The fascinating story of how
early *Homo sapiens*
became modern humans

Wallace (Shaun) Shaunfield

Author's website: www.MyGodYourGod.net

Nealhas Publications
Boerne, Texas

Printed by CreateSpace
Available from Amazon.com and other retail
outlets.

ISBN-13: 978-1512110913
ISBN-10: 1512110914

The cover is a pictorial representation of the story in the book. It begins with the introduction of *Homo sapiens* 200,000 years ago, as shown by the caveman in the bottom-left. The solid line represents civilization. During the early years, there was only a small advancement in civilization. About 10,000 years ago, the Ice Age ended, climates moderated and agriculture began as represented by the early farmer. Then there was a rapid increase in civilization, which continues until this day, represented by the modern man holding books.

To the true scientists who follow the evidence,
wherever it leads.

HUMANS

CONTENTS

ACKNOWLEDGEMENTS

This book is the result of my continuing need to better understand God, after becoming a Christian a short ten years ago. The book was possible because of the support I received from my fellow Christian friends.

In particular, I would like to thank the group who read the draft for content and clarity. They had the difficult task of following my engineer logic in building the story, and they came through with great suggestions. They are Rev. Dr. Ricky Burk, Dr. Paul Griffin, James Glass and Richard (Sandy) Quinn. Special thanks go to the two special people who had the difficult task of correcting my grammar and punctuation. They are DeLana Quinn and Faye Jarrell. I appreciate their patience and correction of the many errors.

PREFACE

When I wrote my first book in 2009, I had a need to discuss human consciousness,[1] and I realized that the early *Homo sapiens* were instinctive driven characters much like their ancestor *Homo* species and not like the thinking *Homo sapiens* of today. I concluded the early *Homo sapiens* did not possess consciousness, and the modern *Homo sapiens* of today do possess consciousness. That raised the key question: When did consciousness first appear in humans? To my surprise, I found only two authors in the field of consciousness studies that even considered the question of when it first appeared.

The first author was Julian Jaynes in 1976 in his famous book.[2] Jaynes argued that consciousness first appeared about 3,000 years ago and based his conclusion on the change in the nature of people in the *Iliad* written by Homer in about 900 to 850 BC. This has been a controversial view, and I do not believe it is supported by the evidence, which shows consciousness appearing at an earlier time. When Jaynes published his book, I became

---

[1] Consciousness as used here is the unique human mental facility as characterized by thinking and numerous attributes including: sense of self, imagination, reasoning, sense of time, language, etc. Chapter 3 is devoted to consciousness.

[2] Jaynes, Julian. 1976. *The Origin of Consciousness in the Breakdown of the Bicameral Mind.* New York: Houghton Mifflin.

interested in consciousness. I had the idea that maybe thinking was, in effect, the two sides of the brain communicating with each other, and that possibly you could build a computer that could think by having two processors communicate with each other in a similar manner. Since computers were not in my field of work in electronic semiconductor components, I did not have the opportunity to pursue this idea. However, I still think there is some merit to the concept.

The second author who looked at the origination of consciousness was Jay Earley, Ph.D., who came very close to what I believe is the actual time full consciousness first appeared.[3] However, Earley had another focus in his work and I do not believe he realized the significance of his conclusion.

This situation prompted me to see if I could determine when consciousness appeared in humans. A look at human history quickly provides a close approximation of this key event. Around 11.5kya,[4,5] the Ice Age[6] ended, climates moderated and the age of agriculture began with humans transitioning from hunter-gatherers to farmers. That was followed by rapid advances in civilization, which has

---

[3] Jay Earley, PhD. 1997. *Transforming Human Culture*. NY: State University of New York Press.

[4] http://www.timelineindex.com/content/view/538. [Accessed: 21July 2007]

[5] kya is the abbreviation for thousand years ago. mya is the abbreviation for million years ago.

[6] The term "Ice Age" used here refers to the last major glaciation that occurred in North America and Eurasia, from 2 million to 11,500 years ago, during the Pleistocene period.

continued until today. This was a monumental change in life on Earth, and it occurred in the past ten thousand years out of the 3.8 billion years that life has existed on Earth. I concluded that consciousness was the necessary ingredient for all this to happen; therefore, I believe consciousness first appeared about 10kya. Other authors were well aware of this change in human behavior, but I am not aware that any of them concluded consciousness was the factor that made it all possible.

The primary goal of this book was to refine the details of the acquisition of consciousness. This has been accomplished partly due to the breakthrough discovery of a new technique in logic I call Non-Evolving Attributes (NEA). It is a rather simple concept but profound and solid. NEA allows us to determine the first time occurrence of certain attributes of early *Homo sapiens* with a high degree of accuracy. It is described in detail in Appendix B.

As I was well into the book, I raised one more question: Were there other attributes that were similar to consciousness in behavior and origin? The answer was a very strong YES, and the result is these other attributes, along with consciousness, are much more important than just the story of consciousness alone. It is the story of how God defined and placed His children, humans, on Earth. Furthermore, we will see how the scientific story of *Homo sapiens* appearing 200,000 years ago, and the story of God placing Adam and Eve on Earth about 6,000 years ago are now in agreement. With that, we now have science and scripture in agreement as you would expect, since the Book of Scripture and the Book of Nature should be in agreement, as they both have the same author. As far, as I know this is the first time this conflict between science and scripture has been adequately resolved.

The story of humans being introduced on Earth is somewhat complicated and detailed, but all of the key points are based on solid evidence and logic. There is very little conjecture in the story.

I recommend your read both Appendices now, as they provide a basis for some of the thoughts that follow. You might not agree with what I say, but at least you will know where I stand on key issues.

1 INTRODUCTION

About 200kya modern humans, *Homo sapiens* (Latin for wise man), first appeared in Africa. *Homo sapiens* are the last surviving species of the *Homo* genus that consists of about 14 earlier species, which are believed to have first appeared about 2.80 to 2.75 mya, approximately the time of widespread tool use and also at the onset of the Ice Age.[1] Compared to the earlier *Homo* species, *Homo sapiens* were more advanced with a larger brain of about 1300 cubic centimeters, and with less of the rugged facial features of earlier species. They appeared to have a somewhat higher level of intelligence as demonstrated by the ongoing advancement in their tools and spear points. It was as if the previous *Homo* species were prototypes of the *Homo sapiens*.

Now consider that today's modern humans are anatomically the same as the first *Homo sapiens*. However, there are some physical differences caused by differences in diet, environment, and climate in addition to some interbreeding between Homo sapiens and ancient humans, the Neanderthals and Denisovans.[2] There is a vast difference

---

[1] Villmore, B. et al. 2015. *Early Homo at 2.8 Ma from Ledi-Gearu, Afar. Ethiopia* [Online]. Available at:
http://www.sciencemag.org/content/early/2015/03/03/science.aaa134 3.abstract?sid=5001d97d-e6cb-4946-89ab-68cbfb2d5c78.

[2] https://en.wikipedia.org/wiki/Archaic_human_admixture_with_modern_humans. [Accessed 7 July 2015].

between the early and modern humans, not in physical characteristics or brain size but instead in brain function and daily activity. Given that the humans today are physically the same as the early *Homo sapiens,* the focus of this book will be on the cognitive capabilities. The first *Homo sapiens* were hunter-gatherers and were primarily instinct driven creatures, the same as their ancestor species. Instinct means that essentially all required behavior is preprogrammed for the events the creature will encounter in their life. The first *Homo sapiens* lived in small clans and were typically on the move in search of food. In contrast, the modern humans are complex, thinking, reflective and creative creatures with the abilities that have made monumental advancements in civilization. And they now live in a complex society along with millions of other people. For the first time in the history of life on Earth, *Homo sapiens* are the only creatures with these unique abilities and lifestyle. While the civilization advances have brought significant improvements in the quality of life, not all peoples enjoy these advancements. In addition, the advances have brought about horrific events, which have led to the death of millions. And these events seem to increase with time.

Until recently, many thought that the only difference between the earlier primates and *Homo sapiens* was in degree, due to higher evolution of the human mind, since both have the same physical structure in the body and brain. Others thought that the monumental difference in degree was sufficient to make humans special. This view has been debated in recent years without resolution. Then in 2014, it was reported that a region of the brain was discovered called the **lateral frontal pole prefrontal cortex,** and it is believed to be unique to humans and may support distinctive cognitive abilities.[3,4] I believe this new evidence strongly supports the view that modern *Homo sapiens* actually are a unique and special creature that are not only different in degree, but also in kind.

The obvious question is: What is the difference between the first *Homo sapiens* and the humans of today? Furthermore, how did this drastic change occur? This book presents my hypothesis that the early *Homo sapiens* were predominately instinctive in their behavior, and the modern *Homo sapiens* have the unique attribute of consciousness and its associated advanced behavior. It tells the story of how early *Homo sapiens* became the modern humans of today. So, the book really is the story of how consciousness originated in *Homo sapiens*. This is an important story; it tells where we came from, and that is of interest to most all of us. I call the period of transition from hunter-gatherers to thinking humans, with full consciousness, the **Sapient Breakout**. Note that when I use the word, "evolution", it is the generic definition of change and not Darwinian Evolution, a specific process of change.

---

[3] Neubert eta al.Comparison of Human Ventral Frontal Cortex Areas for Cognitive Control and Language with areas in Monkey Frontal cortex. Neutron (2014),http://dx.doi,org/10.1016/j.neutron.2013.11.012.
[4] http://www.livescience.com/42897-unique-human-brain-region-found.html.

I first became interested in this transition story when I researched my first book.[5] At that time, I was looking at the attribute of consciousness in humans, and then, realized it might be the key factor to explain the transition to modern humans. In my second book,[6] I again had the need to include a short discussion of this story and, I learned even more about this important event. In addition, answers emerged to several key questions pondered by men for centuries. I soon became more convinced that our consciousness was the root difference between the first *Homo sapiens*, the hunter-gatherers and modern *Homo sapiens*. I realized this important story of human history could be told in a completely different manner.

The archaeological record shows early *Homo sapiens* were clearly instinctive-driven creatures, while other evidence shows consciousness was actually present from the beginning, but not yet expressed. Finally, with the expression of consciousness, we see the emergence of the modern thinking humans of today. As part of the initial study, I raised the key question: When did consciousness first appear in humans? I believe my theory provides the answer to that question.

There is one mystery in the story that adds to its complexity. It is not until looking at evidence at the end of the story and using the newly realized principle of **Non-**

---

[5] Shaunfield, Wallace, 2010. *My God, Your God?*, Boerne, Texas: Nealhas Publications.

[6] Shaunfield, Wallace (Shaun). 2012. *GOD Exists! Ten Evidences for Belief.* Boerne, TX: Nealhas Publications.

Evolving Attributes (NEA)[7] that clearly shows consciousness was present with the early *Homo sapiens*. However, there is little evidence to indicate consciousness was present; therefore, it must have been suppressed and did not start to become fully expressed until after 10kya. This time period is the most important in the story of *Homo sapiens*, as it is the beginning of when we became the complete humans we are today. That raises several questions: Why was consciousness suppressed? What was the mechanism that initially suppressed consciousness and then allowed it to be fully expressed? These questions will be answered in later chapters.

Methodology

This book is based on simple and fundamental facts, which most lay people already know. There are no complex theories or obscure facts, and there is very little conjecture involved. It should be noted that while a lot of human history is used in this study, it is not about human history. Rather, it is a story of how humans evolved from the instinctive early creatures into the modern thinking humans we are today.

The key to uncovering this story is having the right combination of facts along with the right questions that the story of modern humans emerges. It is that fact that allowed this story to be developed by the author, a retired electrical engineer, and one that is certainly out of his career field of

---

[7] See Appendix B for a detailed explanation.

expertise. It is not just the specific knowledge in the field of historical human behavior that is of the only importance, but it also is the experience of doing research in whatever field that allows the story to be discovered. However, I do believe a person educated in fields such as paleontology, biology, archeology or anthropology will add depth to the story and I believe will confirm the conclusions. The story of the origin of modern humans is an intriguing one and has been pondered for many centuries, but none has provided the story as complete as the one presented here. I am not aware of anyone presenting consciousness as the primary difference between the early and modern *Homo sapiens*.

This discussion is a high level analysis in which details are usually omitted. I utilize independent research that has already been done into the past 200,000 years of human behavior, based primarily on archeological evidence. I have considered and included all the evidence I could find even remotely related to the emerging story, including some evidence that at first seemed contradictory. The story is analogous to one of those wooden puzzles with odd shaped, precision pieces that fit together in a unique way to form a perfect cube. Each piece is like one bit of evidence. The fact that each of the pieces fit together so well in the end is an indicator of the truth of the story.

This analysis is based on secular evidence and logical deductions. However, my final conclusions have some spiritual content, which may not sit well with atheists or pure naturalists. I have the view that in scientific research that I will go where the evidence leads and will make no predetermined conclusion concerning the supernatural or any other belief or opinion. Is this not true science? For an in-depth look at this perspective, I refer you to Appendix A, *Science and the Supernatural.*

I was an atheist for 50 years, until I took an objective look at the question of the existence of God. I found an abundance of evidence for God's existence and accepted Christ in 2005. As a result I do not view the supernatural as something forbidden; in fact I expect to see God's intervention with the supernatural at key points in human history. I consider this as logical, scientific thinking; although, I realize some of you might have different opinions, for which I have the utmost respect.

I believe the early investigators of the subject may have been too close to the archaeological record to think with a broader perspective, and this might be the reason they did not consider consciousness, as I have done in this book. Whatever the reason, there is little evidence that consciousness was ever considered as a factor in the transition to modern humans. Consciousness does have a problem in that a universal definition is not accepted by all in the field. There is still much discussion as to what consciousness really is. I will take a brief look at the various approaches to consciousness research to give you an idea of the scope of current understanding of consciousness. In my analysis, I have taken a high-level look at the topic of consciousness and have not considered the lower base level details, such as at the neuron level in the brain. I looked at the solid higher level evidence and then made conclusions from that.

This analysis resulted in much more than just looking at the question of when consciousness first appeared in humans. It also provided a wide variety of answers to other long-term questions about why humans have certain beliefs and attitudes including:

- When and how our conscience was introduced.
- When and how the universal moral code was introduced.
- When and how free will was introduced.
- An inherent concept of a god.

I would point out that I had no idea these spiritual conclusions would result from my analysis. They were just results of the investigation

Following this chapter until the last chapters there will be no reference to anything spiritual; all of the discussion will be secular in nature. Then in the end it will be up to the reader to draw their own conclusions based on the evidence. I do not consider the book to be spiritual in nature, although in the end there are significant spiritual implications.

Peer Review

This work has not been presented to the scientific or theological community for review, and there are reasons for that. First of all, it covers a wide variety of disciplines, including multiple sciences and theology. I am not sure if there is a journal that would consider it appropriate for their publication or maybe I am just not versed in the proper field. Second, the complete story is book length and probably too long for a periodical.

I did consider publishing in an Open-Access publication but chose instead to go directly to a book format, principally because of the length of the document.[8] While publication in a peer-review journal is usually preferred for a new concept, it is not always the way things are done. Therefore, I submit this book for your review and food for thought. I would be very interested in any comments that readers might have. They can be submitted on this book page on Amazon.com in the Review section. Comments are also welcome on my website: MyGodYourGod.net. I will respond to those comments. I believe the ideas of this book will be of interest to those from many different disciplines including the life sciences, paleontology, anthropology, archeology and theology.

Organization of Book

Since the primary source of evidence for the hypothesis presented here is based on the historical behavior of people, the next three chapters will discuss some of the

---

[8] http://www.evolutionnews.org/2013/04/will_open_acces070631.html.

basics of human behavior. Chapter 2 defines consciousness as used in this study. Since consciousness is central to this story, it is important that you understand what I mean by consciousness. Chapter 3 will summarize the basic activities of the brain, mind and a comparison to the modern computer. The brain is one of the most complex organs and is not yet fully understood. I make no claim to be an expert in this area, but I can present some of the basics that affect our behavior. Chapter 4 examines other factors that influence modern human thinking.

Beginning in chapter 5 and continuing through chapter 10, I will look at human activity for the 200,000 year period *Homo sapiens* have been on Earth. This will be broken down into smaller periods of time where human behavior was about the same. Keep in mind I am looking for changes in behavior that indicate a change from the instinctive-driven creature to the modern thinking human we are today. Specifically, I am looking for signs that consciousness is being expressed and also the factors that brought about the change.

Chapter 11 and 12 will look at the process by which consciousness was suppressed and then later expressed.

Chapter 13 will summarize the attributes realized in this study and present what I believe is an accurate definition of the **Complete Human**.

Chapter 14 presents a high level summary of the story of these remarkable creatures we call humans but more importantly, **God's children**.

Summary

In summary, the history of *Homo sapiens* is well known. They first appeared in Africa about 200kya, made minor advances in their hunter-gatherer lifestyle during the initial years. Then, about 10kya, there began a rapid advancement in civilization, which led to the society of humans we are today. The cause for this major change in behavior has never been fully explained. I submit that the acquisition of consciousness is the answer. Specifically, I believe consciousness was present from the beginning, but it was suppressed until about 10kya when the rapid change in behavior began. This book presents my theory of how this all came about.

2 CONSCIOUSNESS

Since consciousness is such an important factor in the model of the origin of modern humans, I believe it is important to accurately define it as used here. Consciousness has been the topic of discussion for centuries among philosophers, scientists and others. However, with all this discussion and debate, there is not a universally accepted definition. How can you define something you do not understand? Part of the problem is we must use our consciousness to think about and define consciousness, and that seems to be a problem for some. Another problem is that consciousness involves our mind, and while great strides have been made in recent years, we still do not yet fully understand how the mind really works.

In this chapter I will look at the various levels of brain investigation, and then describe and define the level of investigation that is most appropriate for this study. When I use the word "consciousness", I am referring to consciousness as defined here. Keep in mind the goal is to have a definition that allows us to make a reasonable comparison of the brain of the early instinctive driven *Homo sapiens* with that of the modern human with full consciousness.

Spectrum of the Consciousness Definition

At this stage of research of the brain, there is a large amount of activity at the very basic level looking at the neuron level of behavior. The accomplishments here are very impressive, and it is through this work that we will eventually gain a complete understanding of the brain. To give you an appreciation of this work, keep in mind that the human brain has about a thousand billion neurons.[1]

Moving to a higher level of investigation, we might look at brain operation at the level of the various components of the brain. There are three main components of the brain; the cerebrum, cerebellum and brain stem.[2] There are about 15 other different parts to the brain and these can be broken down into many other parts, all connected in some fashion with a three dimensional wiring diagram. There is a good understanding of the function of each of these components. What is amazing is that all of the many body functions, plus our intellect, are controlled by the three-pound mass that is the human brain. Humans have created some amazing systems, but none with the degree of complexity and compactness as the human brain.

At this stage of understanding of the human brain, research at these basic levels of investigation is totally appropriate. Only this approach will lead to a better understanding of the brain; however, for this discussion a higher level of focus is needed. Understanding at these fundamental levels adds little to understanding of the tasks at

---

[1]http://www.nlm.nih.gov/medlineplus/ency/anatomyvideos/000016.htm.

[2] http://www.alz.org/braintour/3_main_parts.asp.

hand. What is needed is to work at a high level without consideration of actions at the neuron level. This will become clear as we continue

Keep in mind that the early *Homo sapiens* must have had brains with this high level of complexity, although all of the capability had not yet been realized. It was surely orders of magnitude higher than previous *Homo* species.

For the purpose of this discussion, I have decided on the simplest definition of consciousness, and I believe it may actually be the most accurate definition for being able to reach conclusions about consciousness in the real world, working environment. The difference from other definitions is simply a matter of perspective. This approach is similar to the black-box approach often used in engineering and science.[3] In this case, you look at the object under investigation from an external perspective without regard for the internal workings. This approach is often used when the internal working are unknown or are too complex. By examining the outputs for numerous and varied input situations, you can get a relatively accurate and predictable model of function of the object under investigation. I believe this is an appropriate approach for the considerations in this book. I also believe as more becomes known about the neuron level of the brain, the ideas and concepts developed here will be enhanced.

---

[3] http://en.wikipedia.org/wiki/Black_box.

Much of the following discussion about consciousness was presented in my first book, *My God, Your God?*, and is repeated here for completeness.[4]

Thinking

In the most basic sense, consciousness can be defined as the ability to think. While this may seem to an oversimplification of the definition, the act of thinking is central to all aspects of consciousness, and that is crucial in all discussions of consciousness. One way to put this in perspective is to consider a creature that does not think but rather acts on instinct. Instinctive actions are predominately predetermined by hard wiring in the brain for each situation that normally occurs in their environment. When a situation arises that is not part of the normal environment and outside the realm of the capabilities of the hard wiring, then confusion ensues. Thinking is negligible if even present in their process of taking an action. On the other hand, a thinking creature presented with a similar unfamiliar situation will normally think through the situation, decide on a course of action and survive or even excel. Now, let us look at the other key attributes of consciousness.

Attributes of Consciousness

While the ability to think is the key attribute, the obvious question is: What is thinking? Thinking is not easy to define, but I will try to keep it simple. Thinking is the act

---

[4] Shaunfield, Wallace. 2010. *My God, Your God?* Boerne, Texas: Nealhas Publications.

of considering or visualizing various topics, scenarios, possibilities and options. To get some insight, let us consider what we think about. What we think about is what makes us human and who we are. The key attributes of consciousness and thinking are:

- Sense of self
- Sense of awareness and perception
- Visualizing
- Imagination and creativity
- Reasoning
- Abstract thought and use of symbols
- Language and speaking
- Sense of time
- Long term memory
- Use of external memory
- Ability to generalize
- Learning and adding to knowledge
- Free will

In each of these attributes, thinking by the conscious mind is central to the activity. Now, let us look at each of these items that the mind thinks about, in the conscious state, to get a more complete understanding of thinking.

Sense of self is the feeling of awareness of ourselves and knowing we are a unique entity and we know who we are.

Sense of awareness and perception is the ability to achieve understanding and awareness of our current situation. Humans and animals have a sense of local awareness, but humans also have an additional awareness of distant locations facilitated by our communication abilities.

Visualizing is the act of creating a scene in our mind of an idea, a concept or a spatial situation. It is this act of reducing something in the complex world to a more manageable situation in our mind, which we can then analyze and comprehend. Visualization is closely related to our imagination and creativity.

Imagination and creativity come into play when our minds visualize things past or things that might be in the future. Creativity is the ability to conceive of new ideas, concepts or thoughts that have never existed. Creativity is due to a large extent to the phenomenon emergence.[5] Emergence occurs when a large complex system, such as the human mind, produces not only the expected output, but also a set of different outputs that are radically novel and unexpected. There is no way to predict the many thoughts that will come from the mind when in a creative state.

Reasoning is one of the minds most powerful attributes. It is the ability to seek truth by consideration, logic and a review of the impact of all options.

Abstract thought and use of symbols is one of the most important and fundamental attributes of modern humans. It led to language, writing, mathematics and even the visual arts.

---

[5] Goldstein, Jeffery. 1999. Emergence a Construct: History and Issues. *Emergence: Complexity and Organization.* I(1). Page 49-72.

Language and speaking is tied to abstract thought and use of symbols. Other creatures communicate by sounds and have a language of some kind. However, humans developed symbols in writing that represented sounds that represented thoughts and concepts. Then, combining them, as in writing or speaking communication, the result becomes highly sophisticated and efficient, which greatly enhances the capabilities of humans.

Sense of time is an awareness of the elusive concept of time and then to use it to plan and optimize our activities. Humans often think about the past and the future, and that is one of the main attributes of humans.

Long-term memory is the ability to recall events from the distant past and that allows humans to put the present into perspective.

Use of external memory is a unique human trait. There is both the ability to create memory as in writing, printing or electronic memory, as well as the ability to recall and utilize it. It allows humans to, in effect, have the benefit of memory well beyond their own internal memory.

Ability to generalize is the ability to translate and extend understanding in one situation to another by use of analogies. Understanding in one set of conditions can be transferred to a situation with similar conditions. For example, a parable will present a story that we can relate to our own lives. Mathematics often creates a solution to one problem that we use later on a totally different set of problems with similar conditions.

Learning and adding to knowledge is much the result of the other attributes. The key is learning is a cumulative addition to the collective human knowledge.

Free will is the ability to select an option of our own choosing. Free will is not strictly an attribute of consciousness, but it is closely related and will be discussed in detail in a later chapter.

It should be clear that the sum of these attributes of thinking, in effect, describes our intellect - our cognitive ability. Using and enhancing our intelligence involves the act of thinking. Humans can have numerous disabilities and still demonstrate their intelligences except in the loss of the ability to think. It should be noted that all humans have all these attributes, although some have a higher degree of some attributes such as in memory, imagination and creativity. The question is: Are those attributes present in all humans but not developed, or are they just present at a lower level?

Looking at what humans think about gives us a better understanding of the definition of thinking. Notice that most of the above attributes are closely related and often overlap. Thinking is a complex, multidimensional attribute. At times, it is a process of playing out various scenarios, and then, making a decision of which one to choose. The range of decisions will range from the very simple to the very complex. For example, you may make a decision of what clothes to wear today or what course of study to pursue in college. Other times, there is the act of formulating and then solving a complex mathematical problem. Another action is the recalling of events past and talking about them to friends. Thinking can also be the simple act of watching a movie and becoming part of the plot. Or, it can be the complex act of inventing a new concept to solve a problem.

In examining all these attributes, it is easy to see that they are unique to humans. While our pets sometimes appear to be thinking, they may be to a very limited degree; however, typically, it is a trick that is taught, usually a response to obtaining food.

The most famous case of animals demonstrating animal consciousness is the story of Kanzi, a bonobo, who has undergone extensive training at the Great Apes Trust, in Des Moines, Iowa.[6] Kanzi has demonstrated extraordinary skills in language and human type behavior, at least for a bonobo. He knows about 350 symbols and communicates by pressing an electronic keypad. He also knows the meaning of about 3,000 spoken English words and has composed simple sentences.

However, while these are remarkable feats, Kanzi, if human, would be considered retarded. Many linguists argue that these feats do not constitute language. Gary Pullum, a linguist at the University of California at Santa Cruze says, "I do not believe there has ever been an example of a nonhuman expressing an opinion, or ever asking a question. Not ever."[7]

---

[6] http//www.grateapetrust.org/bonobo/meet/kanzi.php.
[7] http://www.smithsonianmag.com/science-nature/speakingbobnbo.html.

Summary

Volumes have been written on the subject of consciousness, and what I have presented here is an obvious simplification of the subject. However, I believe what I have stated in these few pages captures the essence of consciousness that best fits the purpose in this book. Consciousness is a complex and powerful attribute that makes humans vastly superior to all other creatures on Earth.

Later, we will see how the addition of other unique attributes such as the moral code, conscience, the sense of a god and free will, plus a series of other attributes will make humans complete.

3 BRAIN, MIND, COMPUTER

Dualism

The basic definition of dualism is a condition of being double or a duality, such as mind and matter, good and evil, physical and spiritual.[1] Although the concept originated with the early Greek philosophers, it was René Descartes (1596-1650) who gave the first systematic account of the mind/body dualism.[2] Used here, the definition of mind-body dualism is reduced to mind-brain dualism. The basic concept is the brain is matter and the mind is spiritual or thought and is closely related to our consciousness. For those with a spiritual perspective, the mind is our soul and is independent from the brain. However, the popular view today is dualism is out of favor, and the mind and brain are one in the same. The words, mind and brain, are typically used interchangeably. However, I generally use the brain as the physical entity and the mind as in consciousness or a thinking entity. This is a greatly simplified discussion of dualism and is presented so that you will be aware of the concept. Even a moderate discussion on the philosophy of dualism would be well beyond the scope of this book.

---

[1] http://www.thefreedictionary.com/dualism.
[2] http://serendip.brynmawr.edu/Mind/Descartes.html.

Electronic Computer

The human brain has been considered by many to be a computer, not an electronic based computer, but still a computer. To make this comparison, first look at today's computer properties. Central to each computer is the CPU (central processing unit). The largest commercially available CPU chip in early 2015 had about 4.3 billion transistors on a chip of silicon with an area of 0.84 square inches.[3] Since it takes two transistors to make a switch, there are about 2.1 billion switches in the CPU. In addition, there are other peripheral integrated circuits to complete the basic computer.

The electronic CPU is basically a serial data processor, handling each bit of data in the sequence received. The data rates can be very high, typically in the range of Gbps (1,000 million bits per second). There can be several CPUs on a single CPU chip, processing data in parallel to speed up the computation.

The structure of the CPU and integrated circuit chips is basically a two dimensional electronic circuit, laid out on the silicon chip surface with the semiconductor devices (transistors, resistors and interconnections), fabricated in the third vertical dimension, all within the top one ten thousandth of an inch. The circuit is basically the hardwired instructions in machine code for computation. It has significant repetition and is arranged in functional blocks

---

[3] http://en.wikipedia.org/wiki/Transistor_count. [Accessed: 16 February 2015].

such as memory, computing and timing circuits. With that many components, the circuit is extremely complex.

Creating a CPU is a major team effort involving people such as the overall architect, individual component designers, circuit designers, semiconductor processing designers, computerized circuit simulators, process control people, testing people, and quality control people. Fabrication is typically done in a fully automated, people free, super-clean room. The key to the feasibility of creating such a device is highly dependent on computers used from the modeling of performance, to the layout of the components, to the final testing of such a device.

If you add the volume of the CPU and all of the associated circuits, you will find it is close to the volume of the human brain. Think of the volume of a laptop computer compared to that of the brain.

Just as we have multiple levels of consideration in the computer, we also have similar levels in the brain. For example, the most basic look at a computer might consider the semiconductor device physics of the components involved. Next, we have the basic circuit of the computer. Then, we move up to how we communicate with the computer using assembly programming language, and then move to a more advanced program language, and finally an application program we work with such as MS Word, the program I am using right now. When working with a high level of programming, there is no benefit to even consider the semiconductor device physics.

In a similar manner, as discussed in the previous chapter, we will look at the question of consciousness at a high level of brain activity without any consideration at the neuron level.

Human Brain

The human brain is totally different in structure than the electronic computer. Well-known neuroscientist and Nobel Prize winner, Dr. Gerald Edelman, is opposed to the idea that the brain is a computer because of the difference in wiring.[4] Instead, he sees the brain as a pattern recognizer. But if a computer can be programmed to be a pattern recognizer, does it cease to be a computer?

The brain, while different in structure, has some similarities in function. However, it is a living organism, three to four pounds in weight, located in your skull. It has 30 to 86 billion nerve cells or neurons, which are in effect switches and are connected by about one million, billion connections.[5] The architecture is a massively parallel, electro-chemical signal processor, and while the individual serial connections might not be as fast as the circuits in an electronic computer, the parallel structure can be faster. The brain is extremely complex and can be considered a network of computers or processors, controlling everything from our basic body functions, to our sensory and output functions, to our intellect. The actual circuit of the brain is not fully known. In addition, the human brain is a three-dimensional

---

[4] http://www.consciousentities.com/edelman.htm.
[5] http://consciousness2007.tripod.com/gerald_edelman.htm.

circuit structure making understanding of the actual circuit much more difficult if even possible. We do know that the brain is somewhat flexible, since it can change internal connections, making understanding even more difficult. The brain is very adaptive, and it is believed that no two human brains are the same. I do not believe we even know how to design such a massively parallel computer; we do not fully understand how they really work. Furthermore, we do not know the signal coding system used in the brain.

There are various specialized sections of the brain. The area of most interest here is the cerebral cortex, the wrinkled-looking area at the top and front of the brain. It is part of the cerebrum and is divided into a right and left hemisphere and accounts for about two-thirds of the brain mass. It is believed to be the most recently evolved section of the brain and is where most of our thinking, language abilities and perception occur.[6]

As you can see, the human brain has significantly more processing power than an electronic computer. You have about 86 billion neurons (switches), compared to 2.1 billion switches (more switches mean more power) in addition to the parallel-processing structure, which provides significantly more processing power. The brain can perform many tasks that are not possible with a computer. One is the ability to think. As powerful as today's super computers are, they do not think, and there has not been a single original

---

[6] http://biology.about.com/od/anatomy/a/aa032505a.htm.

idea created by a computer. They can perform massive amounts of logic, but computers do not think yet, if ever.

Note that the apparent discrepancy between the 86 billion and the thousand billion neurons stated earlier is an indication of the level of confidence we have about the brain. Obviously, both are estimates, as no one has counted the actual neurons.

Most knowledge about the brain comes from scans such as MRIs that detect which parts of the brain are active as specific mental tests are given to a live subject, but we do not know the specifics of the actual signals. What these scans show is that while most of the brain activity is in the cerebral cortex during conscious thinking, there is activity throughout the brain.

As mentioned earlier, a newly-discovered region of the brain is tied to the higher-thinking processes.[7] The region, called the lateral frontal pole prefrontal cortex is unique to humans and likely a factor in the language and superior cognitive capability of humans. If this proves to be true, it supports the view that humans really are unique and special creatures.

The brain of any advanced creature is truly a remarkable entity, but the human brain is even more marvelous because of its large computing capability. The capability of the human brain is much greater than the brain of other creatures, partly due to the larger brain size, but also

---

[7] Neubert et al. Comparison of Human Ventral Frontal Cortex Areas for Cognitive Control and Language with Areas in Monkey Frontal Cortex, *Neuron* (2014), http://dx.doi.org/10.1016/j.neuron.2013.11.012.

believed to be due to a different wiring scheme. Considering the computing power, the small size, and the nominal power used, the human brain is the most efficient and powerful computer on Earth. There has been remarkable progress in neuroscience, but given the complexity of the subject, I believe we are still in a primitive stage of understanding how the human brain works.

4 OTHER BEHAVIORAL INFLUENCES

While we normally think that our behavior is controlled primarily by our thinking consciousness, there are many other factors that control our behavior. We often do things automatically without thinking, and that allows us to focus on the unique and probably more important things in our life. In fact, there are probably more automatic actions than conscious actions. These automatic influences include our subconscious, instincts, habits and beliefs. The subconscious is closely related to our consciousness, but is below our sense of awareness. Instinct is the most basic of the attributes controlling our behavior. It is common to all living creatures to some degree. Early *Homo sapiens's* behavior was controlled primarily by instinct and when *Homo sapiens* acquired consciousness, the early instincts were retained. Instincts have declined in importance in controlling our behavior, but they are still present. Habits are an important factor in our lives. We have both good and bad habits. Often, there is not a clear distinction between our subconscious, instinctive and habitual behavior; they are closely related.

In addition to these influences, there are other external influences that affect out behavior. Such influences include: standards, results of innovators, environmental conditions and society's influences.

Subconscious

The human mind can also be looked at in another dimension, that of the conscious and the subconscious mind. The conscious mind is the aware mind, and the subconscious mind is below and out of our awareness. The attributes of consciousness discussed above are primarily attributes of the conscious mind, but not all, as we shall see later.

There are numerous other examples of our subconscious controlling our actions. The actions in sports are a classic example. Athletics train their body and mind to have that perfect golf swing, high jump, swimming stroke and so on. In each of these situations, there is not time to think about the actions; they must be automatic. They become habitual. These types of actions are much faster than those that require thinking. For example, the conscious mind processes data at about 40 bps (bits per second) while the subconscious process at about 40 million bps.[1] Our subconscious is obviously much faster than our active conscious. In addition, there are other significant differences between the conscious and subconscious mind. The conscious mind is volitional and can think abstractly, but can only handle one to three events at a time, while the subconscious mind is habitual, thinks literally and can handle thousands of events at a time.[2] The conscious mind, although seemingly is not as powerful as the subconscious

---

[1] http://lifeboost.hubpages.com/hub/The-Power-of-the-Subconscious-Mind.

[2] http://www.gracefulharmony.com/services/ecode/psychk/convssub/.

mind, has unique and powerful capabilities that make the human different from animals. A comparison of the various differences between the conscious mind and the subconscious mind are listed in Table I.

A classic example of our subconscious in action is the act of driving a car in a repetitive situation such as driving to work. Unless there is an extraordinary event, our subconscious does all the work, making instinctive type decisions of when to accelerate, turn, brake and even what route we take. This example might be considered a learned instinct. We typically do not even have a recall of the event after we arrive. Initially, when we make the first drive, there is a lot of thinking. Which is the best route? How long does it take? In addition, there are all the other details of the drive. After a number of drives, our subconscious takes over, and our mind typically has other thoughts being processed during the drive. Note that our conscious mind can override our subconscious as in the case of something different from the learned event such as an emergency.

Instinct

Instinct defined by the Merriam-Webster online dictionary is: "a largely inheritable and unalterable tendency of an organism to make a complex and specific response to environmental stimuli without involving reason." The key words are inheritable and unalterable. In addition, the properties are the same for all members of a species. It is hardwired and exists without training or experience. We are

Table I The Conscious Mind Versus the Subconscious Mind[3,4,5,6]

Conscious Mind	Subconscious Mind
Our awareness	We are unaware
Generally in control	Takes over when conscious steps aside
Generates ideas and impresses them on the subconscious	Accepts ideas from conscious and accepts them as true
Volitional	Habitual
Inputs from self, environment, subconscious mind	Inputs from conscious mind and our sensory inputs
Creative, analytical and logical	Not as logical, believes everything it is told
Thinks abstractly	Thinks literally
Sleeps	Never sleeps
Short term memory, Approximately 20 seconds	Long term memory, past experiences, attitudes, values, habits and beliefs.
Processes one to three events at a time	Processes thousands of events at a time
Processes 40 bits of information per second	Processes 40 million bits of information per second

[3] http://www.gracefulharmony.com/services/ecode/psychk/convssub/.
[4] http://lifeboost.hubpages.com/hub/The-Power-of-the-Subconscious-Mind.
[5] http://answers.yahoo.com/question/index?qid=20080702213616AABU6mM.
[6] http://www.tonyfahkry.com/subconscious-mind-and-its-impact-on-our-behaviour/.

all familiar with instinct that we have observed in animals. I live in a rural area where there are numerous white tail deer. To avoid danger, the deer have an instinct of freezing, without movement at the sign of danger, such as an approaching car. Then, when it is apparent the danger is too near, they make a rapid movement in a random direction unknown to either the deer or their normal predator. The problem is that the direction of movement is often into the path of the car. Often, they will actually run into the side of the passing car. If they could reason, it would be easy to avoid the cars.

Instinct is an ancient attribute of the brain and the source is not fully understood. The term "instinct" was first used by Wilhelm Wundt in the 1870s.[7] In recent years, the term has fallen out of favor in the field of psychology. However, instinct is clearly a real attribute in most living creatures, including humans. Many investigators have looked at the source of instincts; including Charles Darwin who felt instinct compared favorably with habit in respect to actions, but rejected instincts as the source because habits are not inheritable.[8] Darwin did not present a source of instinct.

Instincts are long-term attributes that surely are passed from old to new species. It is also conceivable that they may be improved by evolution. But the question remains, how did instincts originate in the first place?

---

[7] http://en.wikipedia.org/wiki/Instinct. [Accessed: 3 Mar 2014].

[8] Darwin, Charles, 1859, *Origin of Species*. Chapter VIII. Instinct. St Petersburg, FL. Republished by Red and Black Publishers

When Darwinism, evolution by random, unguided mutations was introduced, it won out over Lamarckism, evolution by a guided process and the inheritance of acquire characteristics.[9] However, work during the past 30 years shows it is possible for acquired traits to be passed on to offspring by the process of epigenetics. In epigenetics, the DNA (deoxyribonucleic acid, the molecule at the nucleolus of each cell, defines the being and how reproduction occurs) is not modified, but rather markers attach themselves to the genome and turn off genes, causing a change in the genetic traits. Could an advantageous habit be the acquired trait that is passed to offspring by epigenetics and then eventually modifies the DNA and becomes a long-term instinct?

Modern humans have instincts the same as early humans and animals and act on them without thinking. Many of our daily actions are the result of instincts that are hard wired in our mind just as in instinctive creatures. Early *Homo sapiens* were guided primarily by their instinct, as their consciousness was not fully realized. Instinct has the property of not changing and of being constant. Some authors believe instinct cannot be overridden by reasoning; however, I side with those who believe it can, at least for certain instincts. As an example, fear is an instinct that we do not override for the sake of survival. However, we can learn how to respond to the fear signal sent to the amygdale, the fast response region of the brain. While the fear stimulus is always sent to the brain, our fear response is learned, and we

---

[9] Turin, George. http://georgeturin.blogspot.com/2013/08/lamarckism-revisited.html. [Accessed: 22 Mar 2014].

also learn how to respond to that stimulus.[10] That explains why some people are fearful of certain situation, while others are not. Fear is just one of many instincts we experience.

When humans acquired consciousness, it was added to instinct and became a much larger force in the modern human. Humans still need and depend on instincts. However, with the hunter-gatherer, instinctive behavior dominated. For example, when food supplies became low, the decision to go out for a new hunt was not the result of a reasoning activity followed by a decision that they should obtain more food. I submit it was due to an instinctive sense of the leader that a hunt was in order, and the hunters of the clan went along without discussion. It is reasonable to assume this type behavior existed for essentially many other activities of the early clans.

Any change in behavior would have required some major external force to be present such as a climate change, movement in the herds, or encroachment by a neighboring clan. They had not realized a capability for reasoning that a change was in order. Without consciousness, the concept of a change by their own volition was not in their being.

Habits

Behavior due to habit is similar to instinct, but it is acquired by one's own experience and learning. Habits emerge because the brain is constantly looking for ways to save effort and in doing so will try to make any routine into a

[10] http://www.actualfreedom.com.au/library/topics/instincts.htm. [Accessed: 21 March 2014].

habit.[11] Just like our subconscious, the habit takes over freeing up our consciousness for thought that only it can perform. Claude Hopkins defined a three-step loop to examine the process of habits in our brain. First, there is a cue, then a routine and finally a reward.[12] An example is seeing a package of cigarettes, then smoking and finally enjoying the nicotine rush.

There is much overlap in activities of our subconscious, instinct and habit. Is driving a car on a routine trip our subconscious or a habit? Maybe the best way to describe the activity is that it is a habit that is carried out by our subconscious brain.

Standards

Standards are typically a unified and an agreed upon method of some activity. Often, the standard is an optimized method, but in other times, the standard is arbitrary. Our modern life is greatly influenced by many different standards, some personal and others global. Standards include definitions on utilities, construction, social behavior, air traffic control and many other areas. Community standards are a necessary factor in having a smooth operation of our societies. Standards can exist for a very long time, but the primary reason is just so that everyone is doing it the same way each time to avoid confusion. In addition, there are quasi-standards that are usually associated with an individual and are just a way of doing something the same each time

---

[11] Duhigg, Charles. 2012. *The Power of Habit*. New York: Random House.
[12] *Ibid*.

without a strong basis. An example might be the way dishes are arranged in the cabinet.

Beliefs

As discussed earlier, change requires reasoning; therefore, without a capability for reasoning, change is difficult if not impossible. An example of this is a group of people with consciousness will adopt a belief system and hold to that belief for centuries. The only way this continues is that there never is an objective reconsideration of the truth of the belief. There never is any question of the belief. With limited consciousness, it is easy to see that the effect of reluctance to change would make the belief even stronger and long lasting. But, it is also important to realize that the adoption of a new belief without consciousness would require a monumental event to change and accept the new belief. It should be noted that some change is due to external forces such as seen in nature, but the actual change by a person requires that the inevitable be accepted and change in behavior is in order, often to survive.

Beliefs are often imposed on others in the group by the ones in control. Those who do not accept the beliefs of the group are often ostracized. Even the new ideas of innovators are often rejected.

When discussing beliefs, it is important to discuss objective and subjective. Objective views are based on facts rather than feelings or opinions, and are not influenced by feelings.[13] Subjective views are based on feelings or opinions rather than facts.[14] While there may be other sources, beliefs can result from an objective or a subjective reason. For example, at about age 17, I decided there was no God. I talked to no one, read nothing and did no research on the subject. I just decided on my own feelings that there was no God and held that opinion for many years. My belief was based on a subjective and irrational reason. Many years later, I decided I would take an objective look at the question of God. I researched the subject and realized there was a wealth of evidence that God was real and changed my belief. This time, I did not depend on my own feeling or beliefs, but kept the analysis objective.

As you look at the beliefs held by humans around the world, you find a broad variety of sometimes similar but often contradictory beliefs. Why is this? It is the dominate source of conflict and war. The reasons are many, including: different interpretation of evidence, subjective consideration of the evidence and customs of unknown sources. In addition, beliefs are formed either subjectively or objectively, based on the evidence available at the time. Later, contrary truths emerge, but the beliefs, both religious and secular, often remains unchanged. Beliefs are often kept for a lifetime and passed down to offspring.

---

[13] http://www.merriam-webster.com/dictionary/objective. [Accessed: 25 March 2014].
[14] Ibid.

Innovators

Some limited change did occur in the early years of *Homo sapiens*. New tools were created and the use of ochre, apparently for body painting, indicated some level of symbolic thinking. How did this come about? I believe the answer for this change is the same as the way change occurs today.

Essentially, all change in our societies is the result of an innovator who is thinking in an unconventional way; thinking out of the box. Today, we typically think of innovators as the engineers, scientists, and artists. However, innovators are present in essentially all fields of endeavor. They are those people who think differently from the normal way of doing things. Education is not a strong factor in identifying innovators. In fact, some of the most creative innovators were without college degrees. You cannot teach creativity. However, education does provide the innovator with tools to analyze and develop their ideas.

The number of people with this capability is a small percentage of the population; I estimated it to be in the range of 0.1 to 1.0 percent for the present time. I suspect the number would be much smaller for the predominately instinctive driven early humans. For the small size African clans, there often would be many generations before an innovator would be present. Even then, if an innovator had a good idea, it is likely it would be rejected just as it often is today. The early innovators were probably the "nerds" of the day. The innovations during this early period were of the type that a single individual could create, such as a new spear point made from bone. While consciousness was suppressed during this early period, there were rare times when it would appear in a limited way in the minds of an innovator. If the idea really was good, then it probably would have been adopted and would have required some limited level of consciousness and reasoning by members of the group. All of the advancements of this period were of this nature, and it is easy to see why, with a small total population and the resulting small number of innovators, there were such small numbers of advancements.

There is one other attribute that is pertinent to the innovator. A person who had realized some low level of consciousness would have had an advantage over others in the clan and likely evolved to the status of a chief or shaman. Shamans were believed to be messengers between the human and the spirit world. As will be discussed later, the concept of a god or gods was a common belief inherent in all humans, but was not expressed until the consciousness was realized. Shamanism appears to be the first predecessor of this belief. There is evidence that Shamanism existed as early as 25,000 BC in Europe and earlier in North Asia.[15] This is about the same time that cave art appeared.

In summary, I believe that innovators, in the very early years, were individuals that were still primarily instinct driven but had some limited level of consciousness that allowed them to be creative. Their level of consciousness probably was higher than other members of the group, and

---

[15] http://easternhealingarts.com/Articles/shamanism.html.[Accessed: 1 Jan 2014].

this ability allowed them to initiate the changes we see through our history. Consciousness was present in a very limited degree and was far from full consciousness.

Free Will

A discussion of the mind and manner in which it makes decisions would not be complete without a discussion of free will. Free will is the ability to make choices free from external forces. It is clear that external forces may influence our decisions, but in the end, we are free to choose. And there are times when things, such as political control, may restrict our ability to act as we choose, but we can always still think as we choose. Free will is one of the most important factors in our makeup. It has allowed humans to explore new ideas and territories and in doing so, humans have achieved the monumental results we have seen over the past 10k years. Free will obviously requires the ability to think with some level of consciousness to have meaning.

However, the existence of free will is one of the most debated topics in the field of consciousness. Many do not accept its existence. Susan Blakemore interviewed 18 experts in the field of consciousness and asked if they thought humans had free will.[16] The results were: 44% answered "Yes", 33% answered "No", and 22% answered "Not sure". Less than half thought we actually have free will. Author, Eddy Nahmias, author of *Why We Have Free Will*, understands the situation and provides a proper argument

---

[16] Blakemore, Susan. 2006. *Conversations on Consciousness*. New York: Oxford University Press.

that humans do have free will.[17] Another author, Sam Harris, in his book, *Free Will*, claimed humans do not have free will.[18] His conclusion was based on his belief in the philosophy of determinism and the results of a famous experiment by Benjamin Libet.[19]

Is free will real? What is the truth? What is the evidence? Let us first look at the work of neurologist, Libet. During the 1970's, Libet performed experiments into the nature of free will. Subjects were instructed to flex their wrist and then three times were recorded.

1. W, the time of a conscious decision to perform the action.
2. RP, the readiness potential, or the start of the brain activity to perform the action, determined by electrodes connected to the brain.
3. M, the actual time of the action.

The results were surprising. You would expect the sequence of events to be W followed by RP and then M. Instead, Libet observed that RP occurred first, followed by W, delayed by 350-400 ms (milliseconds), and then M about 550 ms after W. In other words, the conscious awareness of the action began to occur 350 ms after activity began in the brain to initiate the action. That suggested the conscious

---

[17] Nahmias, Eddy, 2015. Why We Have Free Will. *Scientific American*. Jan. 2015.

[18] Harris, Sam. 2012. *Free Will*. New York: Free Press.

[19] http://www.centenary.edu/attachments/philosophy/aizawa/courses /intros2009/libetjcs1999.pdfhttp://www.centenary.edu/attachments/ph ilosophy/aizawa/courses/intros2009/libetjcs1999.pdf.

brain was not responsible for the action and to some people, it meant that free will does not exist. I am surprised that after all these years, some still hold to this erroneous view. I believe there is an error in interpretation. First of all, it should be obvious that if the conscious mind did not initiate the action, then the subconscious must have, indicating it had free will. To me, it is clear that the conscious mind, due to the repetitious nature of the task, quickly delegated it to the subconscious mind. The subconscious mind initiated the action and informed the conscious mind of the action a few moments later. Since our consciousness is composed of the combination of the conscious and subconscious minds, and if the subconscious has free will, then is it not true that our consciousness has free will?

Also, note that the Libet's experiment was performed in a quiet, non-stressful environment of the laboratory. If the tests were to be repeated in a stressful environment, I believe the conscious mind would have maintained control, and we would see the originally anticipated order of events.

It is interesting to note Libet did not believe his experiments showed there was no free will. He even showed the conscious mind was able to veto the final action before it occurred. This solved the moral problem that if man is not aware of his actions, then he should not be held accountable. Libet made an interesting statement at the end of the above referenced paper: "Given the speculative nature of both determinist and non-determinist theories, why not adopt the view that we do have free will (until some real contradictory evidence may appear, if it ever does)."

Next, let us look at the philosophy of determinism, the philosophical idea that every event or state of affairs, including every human decision and action, is the inevitable and necessary consequence of antecedent states of affairs.[20] I believe this idea, which has been debated for centuries, comes about from observations that many things, such as those predicted by natural law are deterministic; therefore, the belief that everything is deterministic. We depend on natural laws being deterministic; otherwise, none of the machines in our society would work, nor could we expect gravity would keep us attached to Earth. However, there are many non-deterministic things in nature that are totally unpredictable such as, noise, randomness and events under Chaos theory. A classic example of a random event is the simple flip of a coin. In the design of a scientific experiment or a new product, there is heavy dependence on the deterministic laws of nature; however, the non-deterministic laws of nature must also be factored in and avoided in the design.

The human mind is a classic example of realizing unexpected results based on the theory of emergence.[21] As stated earlier, emergence has the property that in very complex systems, we not only get the expected results, but also novel and unpredictable results. I believe this is the

---

[20] http://www.informationphilosopher.com/freedom/determinism.html.
[21] Goldstein, Jeffery. 1999. Emergence a Construct: History and Issues. *Emergence: Complexity and Organization*. I(1). Pp. 49-72.

source of our imagination and new ideas and concepts. How does free will fit into the theory of determinism? Imagine a line representing the spectrum of free-will options, where the very left point represents a totally deterministic situation, and the very right point represents no constrains on free will. On the left, there would be no free will, but this is not a realistic situation because of the non-deterministic nature that exists with humans. At the point on the right, we would have total free will; however, there would be no input data on which to base decisions. Any decision here would be a total wild guess and have little value. Therefore, it should be clear that free will does exist somewhere along the center of the line, not limited by determinism, but also requiring some external information that influences the decisions to be made.

I would also point out that determinism is a random process without purpose and it cannot explain the purposeful advancements made over the past 10k years. Free will is integral to most world views, and I believe is required for the progress made by mankind. Advancement absolutely will not happen if guided by a random process. Much of popular philosophy is based on humans having freedom including freedom of thought and action. There should be no doubt that humans do have free will.

Conclusion

We have seen that human behavior is complex based on our consciousness, subconscious, instincts, habits, standards, beliefs and our free will. I believe there is much overlap in each of these attributes. The basic premise of the model in this book is based on behavior, before and after the realization of consciousness, with the instinct dominating before and consciousness dominating after. What about the other attributes? As we shall see later, consciousness did show up in a limited amount before the Sapient Breakout along with habits and beliefs. Instincts are still present in modern humans, although it is often overridden by the other attributes.

Finally, we typically think that the modern human is defined by the consciousness and all of those noble attributes – thinking, creativity, reasoning, language, learning, etc. We also like to think we are objective. However, we would be incomplete and totally ineffective without our subconscious, instincts, habits and belief. Imagine getting up each morning in a totally objective mode without any of our daily tasks predetermined. Without these background attributes, we would have to objectively decide every action to be followed each day. We would not get much done.

We like to think we are objective; however, just how many topics are really still open for objective consideration? Unless you are making a major change in your life, there are probably no important topics still open. For example, consider the driving to work. If we had to make each and every decision in that activity, it would take much longer than having our subconscious take care of the driving. I believe that when we say we are objective, we mean that if some important potential change were to arise, we would consider it objectively.

5 ACQUISITION OF CONSCIOUSNESS

We know that everyone on Earth today has the attribute of consciousness as defined in Chapter 3. And yet, when we look at the early *Homo sapiens* we do not see this attribute, at least to the extent we see today. Therefore, this attribute must have been acquired sometime in the period between 200kya and the present. When did that happen and how did it happen? Also, one must ask: How did everyone on Earth end up with the same identical attribute of consciousness? This is especially perplexing considering this attribute is common in groups of people who have been separated from each other by thousands of miles and thousands of years. The answer most often give by atheists is that consciousness evolved, meaning Darwinian Evolution.

However, it can be shown consciousness could not have evolved based on the principal of Non-Evolving Attributes (NEA), which is described in Appendix B. Furthermore, NEA can provide answers to the above questions. This is a very powerful tool in determining original values of attributes at the beginning of a branching process.

The principle of NEA states: When you have populations that are isolated by distance and/or time, and all have evolved from a common ancient ancestor through many different branches, and where each member of the population has an identical attribute, then it can be said that attribute did not randomly evolve, for if it did evolve in any one branch it would have had to evolve the same in all branches, and that is essentially impossible. If the attribute did not evolve, then the original ancestor must have had the same identical attribute as that of the members of today. You can see the power NEA has in determining characteristics of ancient beings.

In today's world, since every human has consciousness, the principle of NEA says that consciousness did not evolve but was present in the first of the *Homo sapiens*.

This is profound. Consciousness and all of its many attributes just appeared in the new *Homo sapiens* without any natural explanation. We have ruled out any form of random evolution, and to further support this, there was no Darwinian mechanism for consciousness to have evolved. There was no advantage to these simple creatures. **The event of the first humans acquiring consciousness was clearly supernatural.**

There is much more to the story of humans acquiring consciousness. It involves a large set of other human attributes were also acquired with consciousness and it is this total set of attributes that define the complete human. This is discussed in Chapter 13.

Earlier, I indicated the original *Homo sapiens* did not demonstrate consciousness and instead were clearly instinctively driven creatures. **That means consciousness initially must have been suppressed until a later date.**

This is supported by strong evidence presented in Chapter 11. It is the acquisition of consciousness and then the suppression that makes this story so intriguing.

6 EARLY AFRICAN PERIOD

Introduction

We will now look at the evidence of consciousness in the history of *Homo sapiens*. At the time *Homo sapiens* first appeared, it is reasonable to assume that they were principally instinctively driven, hunter-gatherers just as their ancestor species had been. They were anatomically the same as the modern human of today, but how did their mental capabilities compare? They were somewhat more advanced than their ancestors, but did they think, and what was the level of thinking compared to humans of today? We saw in the previous chapter that consciousness did not evolve but was present in the earliest *Homo sapiens*, although suppressed. Does the evidence from the history of *Homo sapiens* support this concept?

Earlier, I discussed consciousness as we know it today, a time where we have recorded human history. Unfortunately, the time we are interested in here is before recorded history; therefore, the task will be difficult. Volumes have been written on the fascinating prehistoric history of humans, but all I want to do is get some understanding of their mental or consciousness capability, and I will do that by looking at how they lived and what they did. Again, the summary of this investigation will be short, but I believe that we can get a relative level of their consciousness, so that a reasonable comparison can be made. Keep in mind that the subject of this book is the transition of the early *Homo sapiens* to the modern human of today.

Relationship to Other Species

Homo sapiens appeared nearly 200kya. The oldest known fossils date back to 195kya and were found at Herto, Ethiopia.[1] *Homo sapiens* are the most advanced of the *Homo* genus, which first appeared about 2.8 mya and consists of about 14 different species. All are now extinct except for *Homo sapiens*.[2] One characteristic of *Homo sapiens* is a large cranial capacity. Only the Neanderthal's is slightly larger, and is believed due to their larger bulk. The *Homo neanderthalensis* is the most recent of species before *Homo sapiens*, and they died out about 24kya. About 40-60kya, *Homo sapiens* migrated into Europe, the primary site of Neanderthals; therefore, there was a period of coexistence of around 25ky. There is evidence of interbreeding during this period, so it is very likely you have some Neanderthal DNA.[3] It is thought that *Homo sapiens* and Neanderthals have a common ancestor of

---

[1] Brown, Frank and Siegel, Lee. 2005. *The oldest Homo sapiens*[online]. University of Utah. Available at: www.eurekalert.org/pup_releases/2005-02/uou-toh0211o5.php. [Accessed: 4 May 2013].

[2] This information is available at many web sites such as: *Homo*. Available at : en.wilkipedia.org/wiki/Homo.[Accessed: 27 Nov. 2013].

[3] Zimmer, Carl, 2013. Interbreeding With Neanderthals, Discover Magazine [online]. Available at: www.discovermagazine.com/2013/march/14-interbreeding-neanderthals#UpZi69JDv0c. [Accessed: 27 Nov. 2013].

Homo heidelbergensis, assuming Darwinian Evolution was at work, which might not be the case.

Recently, another *Homo sapiens* creature, the Denisovan, has been discovered.[4] In 2008, the finger bone of a young female was unearthed in the Denisova Cave in southern Siberia. DNA extracted from the bone showed it was neither Neanderthal nor *Homo sapiens*. Very little is known about the Denisovan, but some of their DNA has been detected in the human DNA.

In addition, there have been other archaic *Homo sapiens* species here on Earth that coexisted with *Homo sapiens*. One is the Red Deer People of China, which existed as recently as 11.5kya.[5] Another is the Hobbit like human, about the size of a three year old, which was discovered on a remote Indonesian island and believed to have lived as recently as 13kya.

The estimated number of total species of life identified and living on Earth today is about 8.7 million, and this only includes about 20% of the species. This means that there are in the neighborhood of 40 to 50 million different

---

[4] *Why Am I Denisovan?*.National Geographic. Available at: https://genographic.nationalgeographic.com/denisovan/. [Accessed: 6 December 2013].

[5] Archaic Humans. 2013. Available at: http://en.wikipedia.org/wiki/Archaic_humans. [Accessed: 9 December 2013].

species currently on Earth.[6] We *Homo sapiens* are just one of these species.

Be aware that I am only touching the surface of the fascinating history of early *Homo sapiens* species and much more information is available.

Prehistoric Technology

Relics, typically those stone and bone items that have survived the ravages of time, provide a unique window into the technology of early humans. It is likely they also used items of wood, but very few items have survived. The earliest stone tools date back to 2.6Mya, using the Oldowan tool tradition,[7] which used some minor flaking to produce a sharp edge. By 1.76Mya, the technology had advanced to the Acheuilian tool tradition, which utilized large flakes to shape the tool. Tools of the era included the new handaxe and other large cutting tools.[8] The *Homo sapiens*, when they appeared about 200kya, adopted the current tool stone technology, which was fairly well established. Beginning 75kya, we see a series of advancements beginning with the Mousterian technology, the Aurignacian in 33kya, the Gravettian technology in 27kya, the Solutrean technology in

[6] Sweetlove, Lee. 2011. *Number of Species on* Earth *Tagged at 8.7 Million.* http://www.nature.com/news/2011/110823/full/news.2011.498.html. [Accessed: 23 Jan 2014].
[7] http://humanorigins.si.edu/evidence/behavior/tools/early-tools. [Accessed: 15 Feb. 2104].
[8] Ibid.

21kya and the Magdalenian technology in 17kya.[9] Each of these tool technologies represented a slight improvement over the previous technologies.

Cave Living

Caves are dominant archeological sites for the evidence of the period. There is a concentration of relics found in caves. I believe there are two reasons: 1) caves were a natural place for concentration of activity due to the shelter they provided compared to the many more open sites for gathering, and 2) the caves provided protection for the artifacts left by the early inhabitants, while those left in open sites may not have survived or would be more difficult to find. Most all caves were near to either the ocean or rivers.

Next, I will discuss the evidence of consciousness that was found in a sample of cave sites during the period from 200kya to 10kya, starting with the oldest site.

- **Pinnacle Point** PP13B is a cave located in the coastal cliffs near Mossel Bay, on the southern coast of South Africa. It was occupied by *Homo sapiens* as early as 164kya until about 45kya.[10] Excavations show the first consumption of shellfish, the first evidence of heat treatment of rock to make stone tools, and the use of red

---

[9] http://anthro.palomar.edu/homo2/mod_homo_5.htm. [Accessed: 13 Feb. 2014].

[10] Blake, Edgar, 2008,
http://archive.archaeology.org/0803/abstracts/letter.html [Accessed: 18 Jan. 2014]

ochre for use in body painting.[11] There was also evidence of a capacity for symbols and language, but this cannot definitely be attributed to the earliest inhabitants.[12]

- **Blombos Cave** is located on the Southern Cape coast of South Africa.[13] The early indication of shell fishing and fishing has been dated to as early as 140kya. Significant findings are 75,000 year old ochre engraved with abstract designs and 80,000 year old bone tools.

- **Klasies River Caves** are a group of caves found on the Tsitsikamma coast of South Africa near the Klasies River and are believed to have been occupied as early as 125kya.[14] Evacuations show the people ate shellfish, antelope, seals, penguins and unidentified plant food that had been roasted in hearths. There is also evidence that the inhabitants only stayed in the caves for a few weeks at time.

- **Howieson's Poort Shelter** is a small rock shelter (cave) near Grahamstown in South Africa. It was inhabited roughly between 68.5kya and 59.5kya.[15] This site provides early evidence of human symbolism, and various stone tools and points.

---

[11] http://en.wikipedia.org/wiki/Pinnacle_Point. [Accessed: 18 Jan. 2014].

[12] Blake, op. cit.

[13] http://en.wikipedia.org/wiki/Blombos_Cave. [22 Jan. 2012].

[14] Hirst, K. Kris,
http://archaeology.about.com/cs/humanorigins/a/klasiesriver.htm.
[Accessed: 18 Jan. 2014].

[15] http://en.wikipedia.org/wiki/Howieson's_Poort_Shelter [Accessed: 11 Feb. 2014].

These four cave sites are typical and significant of the culture that existed in Africa following the emergence of *Homo sapiens* in Africa. There were many caves at other sites in Africa during this period. It is clear these people had some level of consciousness to be able to do the things they did. So, how did a predominately instinctive group of people do the things that required consciousness? I believe it was much like today, in that most new things are due to a very few individual innovators who broke out of the instinctive mold and thought "outside the box." On rare occasions, an innovator came along and did things such as body painting with ochre or developed a new spear point out of bone.

One thought is that cave living would have been easier than living outside and more "leisure" time would be available and more conducive to consciousness thinking.

During the early African period, we see the presence to a limited degree the attribute of consciousness. It was required to bring about the things like using red ochre for symbolic body painting and making bone tools and points. It is interesting to note that essentially all advancements were common to all locations, indicating communication between locations.

Considering the long time, 130,000 years, and the relatively small number of inventions and the small size of each invention, they were surely introduced by lone innovators. They were few and far between. Why did this small number of innovators possess the consciousness required for the new idea? It was as if while the dominate behavior was instinctive, there was an underlying presence of consciousness in the people. Then, on rare occasions an individual would break away from the tradition of no change, limited consciousness would appear and a new idea would be born. So, while consciousness during this period was suppressed, it was not total suppression, and creativity occasionally appeared. Assuming consciousness was suppressed, the question then is: How was the suppression removed? We will look at that question in a Chapter 12.

It should be noted that while we see evidence of limited consciousness, the indicated level of consciousness at the end of this period is not significantly different than that at the beginning; it did not appear to significantly change during a period of over 100,000 years.

In summary the key facts from the early African period include:

- The early *Homo sapiens* clearly were hunter-gatherers.
- Limited signs of consciousness appeared in the small number of innovators.
- The advancements made during this early period are minor, and while the improvements were the result of rare events of limited consciousness, I believe this supports the concept that these people were primarily instinctively driven.

7 THE MIGRATION PERIOD

A key piece of the puzzle of the transitions to modern humans is their migration throughout the world. It began 50 to 70 kya with the initial migration out of Africa, and by 10kya all the continents of the earth had been populated by *Homo sapiens*, including the Americas for the first time by any of the *Homo* species. A method for tracking the migration of early humans has been developed using the human DNA, and it gives a unique insight into the migration of early humans.

The Genographic Project

Spencer Wells, PhD., in his book, *The Journey of Man*,[1] and Stephen Oppenheimer, in his book, *The Real Eve*,[2] outlined the technique whereby it was possible to map the path of *Homo sapiens* as they migrated and eventually covered the earth.

The National Geographic Society Genographic Project, a team led by Dr. Spencer Wells, mapped the markers and migrations paths, so an individual can have their

---

[1] Wells, Spencer. 2002. *The Journey of Man*. New York: Random House Trade Paperbacks.
[2] Oppenheimer, Stephen. 2003. New York: *The Real Eve* Carroll & Graf Publishers.

DNA tested to determine the migration path of their ancient ancestors out of Africa.

The DNA molecule is at the nucleus of every cell in our body. It has the shape of a twisted ladder with about ten rungs for each full twist. The rungs are base pairs consisting or four possible chemicals, Adenine, Guanine, Cytosine and Thymine (or A, G, C, and T for short). It is the sequence of the AGCT chemicals and sequence of the rungs that forms the DNA code of each cell and life itself. There are about three billion bases or rungs that define the 20,000 genes of the human body. Occasionally, when the cells divide there is a mutation in the form of a misspelling in the chemicals on a rung. One form of mutation is harmless and shows up in the Y-chromosome in the male or the mitochondrial genome (mtDNA) in the female. The Y-chromosome marker is passed down to the male offspring, and the mtDNA marker is passed down to the female offspring. The markers are passed down to all subsequent generations and exist in people living today.

With migrations, a group of humans would move to a new region and settle down for an extended period. While the early humans did not form villages, they still tended to stay in the same region. These early regions of the hunter-gatherers would eventually become settlements, villages and towns. After a period of time, the harmless mutation would appear in either the Y-chromosome of every male or the mtDNA of every female in that region. These mutations or markers would then be passed down to every subsequent male or female offspring. That marker then became uniquely identified with that region. The amazing thing is that people today still live in many of the original regions and have these unique DNA markers for that region.

Then, the process would be repeated, a group would move on, a new region would be formed, and a different set of markers would eventually appear for the new region. As the total Earth was populated, different markers for each settlement would be created, and it was possible to map these unique markers for settlements around the world. By examining the markers in your DNA, you would know your ancestors spent some time in which settlements and you could then trace the path of your ancestors as they migrated out of Africa. The original Genographic Project by the National Geographic Society in 2005 had identified about 48 markers (24 Y-chromosome and 24 mtDNA) of specific locations around the world. If your ancestors went through any of these marker locations and spent some time there, then they would have picked up these markers, and they are in your DNA today. Participants in the project send in a sample of their DNA obtained by cotton swabbing the mouth and then that would be tested to identify the markers present in their DNA. The approximate date for each marker was also provided. From these markers, you would then know the migration path of your ancient ancestors as they migrated out of Africa.

In 2012, the second phase, Genographic 2.0, was launched. The second phase has an expanded set of 10,000

Y-chromosome and 3000 mtDNA markers.[3] In addition, this new program identifies any Neanderthal and Denisovan genes you might have. It should be noted that other organizations also do DNA testing, but none is as complete as National Geographic for the genetic location markers. More details of the Genographic Project are available on their website.[4]

Earlier, there was an alternate theory that stated *Homo sapiens* evolved at multiple locations (Multiregional model) around the world; however, this DNA technology clearly shows that humans evolved from only Africa (Out of Africa Model).[5]

The Migration

Although *Homo sapiens* first appeared nearly 200kya in Eastern Africa, they did not immediately migrate out of Africa. The probable reason is the path north was blocked by the impassible Sahara desert at that time. Their initial move was to the south about 100kya as indicated by mtDNA markers and 60kya as indicated by Y-chromosome markers. The migration out of Africa began about 50 to 70kya.

A sample of the time of settlement for various locations around the world along with their unique Y-

---

[3] https://genographic.nationalgeographic.com/faq/about-project/ [Accessed: 2 Feb. 2014].
[4] https://genographic.nationalgeographic.com/ [Accessed: 15 Jan. 2014].
[5] Oppenheimer, op. cit. page xx.

chromosome markers ID is shown in Table II.[6] Similar data exists for the mtDNA markers of the female.

The migration that populated the world was often controlled by the climate. At times, various paths were blocked by extreme temperatures, or conditions at their current location became unbearable. Migration was also affected by the availability of food resources and often, the moves followed the migration of the great herds.

Table II Time of Settlement

Location	Marker	time (kya)
Southern Africa	M91	75
Out of Africa	M168	70
Australia	M130	50
Middle East	M89	50
South East Asia	M175	30
Europe	M170	20[7]
Spain	M253	15
South America	M3	10

It should be noted that essentially all of the migration was done during the Ice Age, when the sea levels were

---

[6] Literature from Genographic Projects 1.0, 2.0, 2009, 2005.

[7] It should be noted that mtDNA shows a date into Europe of 40kya and archeological evidence indicate a date as early as 45kya—see Wilford, J. N. 2011. Fossil Teeth Put Humans in Europe Earlier than Thought. NYTines.com. [Accessed: 7 Mar 2014].

significantly lower, allowing the formation of land bridges. The most notable was between Siberia and Alaska that allowed the population of the Americas. Another example is the link between Asia and Australia. While there no complete land bridge, the lower sea level exposed much land and that reduced the distance across the sea making it easier for the early Aborigines to make the crossing. The Aborigines were the among the world's earlier mariners.[8]

It is interesting to note that while the times of 10kya to 75kya are long compared to our life span, they are very short compared to age of the universe or the time life has existed on Earth. The migration led to the population of the earth, including every continent, and lasted only about 65ky. The fact that the whole world was populated for the first time is an indication of the curiosity and resourcefulness of *Homo sapiens*. This is an indication of a higher level of consciousness. While they had a higher level of consciousness, they were still predominantly instinctive creatures.

It is also interesting to note that while there was some interaction between neighboring groups, the distant groups were isolated from each other until the period of exploration that began with the Viking's travel to North America in the 980s.[9] Following that, we have Marco Polo and his travels to China and Far East in 1271.[10] Then,

[8] http://en.wikipedia.org/wiki/Prehistory_of_Australia. [Accessed: 5/28/2015].

[9] http://en.wikipedia.org/wiki/Norse_colonization_of_the_Americas.

[10] http://library.thinkquest.org/4034/polo.html.

beginning with Columbus in 1492, we have the great sea explorations that finally united the earth's populations that had been separated for thousands of years. This long period of separation of the various populations is an important element of the Origins of Modern Humans model and will be discussed later.

Population History

Knowledge of the population of the early humans would be useful, but as you might expect, we do not know it for the very early years. We only have the best estimates of experts. Furthermore, there are limited estimates for dates before the Sapient Breakout. It is estimated that the world population before this time stabilized at around three million people based on the hunter-gatherer lifestyle.[11] It is also estimated that during this early period, the total world population never exceeded 15 million.[12] One reference lists the population around 70kya as low as 2,000, at the start of the out of Africa dispersal.[13] Another reference lists the population around 70kya at one million, quite a difference.[14] I tend to believe the higher estimate is more accurate based on earlier estimates.

---

[11] http://paleodiet.com/life-expectancy.htm . [Accessed: 14 Feb. 2014]

[12] Tellier, Luc-Normand. 2011. *Urban World History: An Economic and Geographical Perspective.* Québec. Presses de l'Université du Québec, eBook.

[13] http://www.sciencedaily.com/releases/2008/04/080424130710.htm [Accessed: 13 Feb. 2014].

[14] http://au.answers.yahoo.com/question/index?qid=20130408171608AA4X2bb. [Accessed: 13 Feb. 2014].

For the years following the Sapient Breakout, the estimates get much closer. Common values of world population are about four million with a range of 1 – 10 million.[15]

The key thing to understand is not the actual number, but rather that the population was very low compared to today's numbers. An even more important way to look at population is the density per area, rather than the total number. We can calculate the density knowing the earth's habitable land area, which today is about 24,642,000 square miles or 15.8 billion acres.[16] However, in the time before the migration out of Africa, only African land can be used. Since Africa has about 11,600,000 square miles and assuming 30% is unusable, then usable area is 8,120,000 square miles. Assuming a population of one million, 70kya, would result in a population density of 8.12 square miles per person. If you have a clan size of 20 individuals, then the area for the clan would be 162 square miles. Since the distribution is probably not uniform, you would have some bunching of population, but, even so, there would be a strong sense of isolation. Anyone living today and transported to that time would have a feeling of loneliness.

Assuming a population of five million at the time of the migration out of Africa, the population density would

---

[15]   https://www.census.gov/population/international/data/worldpop/table_history.php. [Accessed: 13 Feb. 2014]

[16] http://www.zo.utexas.edu/courses/THOC/land.html. [Accessed: 13 Feb. 2014].

have increased five-fold to about 32 square miles per clan, still a large number.

Given the isolation and the abundance of land, it is reasonable to assume that wars between the small clans over land would have been rare. The exception might have been a battle for a special location such as a choice cave.

Conclusion

I believe it is clear that the humans of this period were still hunter-gatherers with behavior controlled by instinct. But they had a small amount of curiosity from a low level of consciousness, probably in the leaders-innovators of the clan.

This period begins with the initial migration out of Africa, about 70kya, and continues until all of the earth was populated by about 10kya. This was the first time that any *Homo* species had migrated into the Americas. It is believed that the main driving force for the speed and magnitude of the migration was the earth's climate.[17] One would expect that a group of people who were adverse to change (as we will see later) would require some compelling force to make them move. However, given that they knew they had to move, I believe curiosity and intellect of the early humans might have come into play, and that could have led them into the Americas.

Markers on the DNA have been invaluable in tracing the path humans took in their migration path. It is

---

[17] www.pbs/newshour/indepth_coverage/science/dna/timeline.html. [Accessed: 11 Nov 2013].

interesting that humans existed in Africa for 130,000 years, and then, when they began to leave, they went to the far reaches of the earth in only 60,000 years. I believe it is also fascinating that people today still live in the same location of the original settlers, their ancestors of 70kya ago. I believe this shows the strong reluctance to change, which is still present today. The good news is that fact allows the DNA migration system to work.

While there was some minor advancement in tools during this period, it is really noted for the vast migration. A key point is the societies that eventually settled in the various locations around the world were separated from each other by thousands of miles and years. It was not until the periods of exploring, which began about 1kya that humans were reunited.

The key bits of information from the migration period include:

- The people were still hunter-gatherers and instinctive driven.
- Limited signs of consciousness appeared in the curiosity that caused the people of this period to migrate to the all parts of the world for the first time in history.
- These people showed a level of adaptability higher than any other creature as they encountered all the variations in climate, food and terrain around the world. Is this not another sign of limited consciousness?

8 EARLY CHANGE PEROD

Prior to the major change in human behavior that began about 10kya, there were several significant early changes, which preceded them. Two of these activities are art, which began to appear about 35kya in Europe and construction of a temple complex at Göbekli Tepe, which began about 11.6kya. While these developments did not indicate the inhabitants had realized full consciousness, they were more advanced than the earlier hunter-gatherers and were a sign of things to come.

European Art

Homo sapiens first arrived in Europe about 40 to 60kya. Shortly after, the first art appeared, indicating some higher level of consciousness. I discuss the European art because it has unique and unusual attributes that add to the understanding of the story of the emergence of modern humans. Be aware art also appeared in most other parts of the world, but none were as advanced as that which first appeared in Europe.

Venus Figures

Some of the most famous art objects of the period are the numerous Venus figures that were made around

35kya to 10kya and found throughout Europe.[1] They were hand-size carvings of a nude woman with exaggerated breasts and buttocks. There were other figurines; however, the Venus versions were clearly the most abundant. The fact that the figures are found throughout Europe indicates the level of communication in the area. The figurines were crafted from various materials including: soft stone, bone, ivory or formed and fired clay. Their purpose is unknown but ranges from a fertility icon, to a religious figure, to pornographic imagery.[2] As there are no other artifacts of religious meaning, I do not believe religion was the purpose. Because of the emphasis on the female figure over such a long period of time and not a random selection of various other objects, it appears they had some specific purpose in mind. It indicates a higher level of consciousness; however, the focus on just the female figure indicates it was still limited. Other art objects included carvings on stone, animal bone and tooth carvings.

Keep in mind that the people of this era were still hunter-gatherers and, I believe, were still primarily instinctive driven characters; although, higher level thinking was beginning to appear in a limited degree.

---

[1] http://en.wikipedia.org/wiki/Venus_figurines. [Accessed: 22 Feb 2014].

[2] https://www.boundless.com/art-history/prehistoric-art/the-paleolithic-period/venus-figurines/. [Accessed: 7 Mar 2014].

European Cave Art

One of the most fascinating creations in human history is the paintings on the cave walls in Europe. Beautiful paintings, primarily of animals, appeared on the walls of caves in Spain and France shortly after *Homo sapiens* arrived. The earliest known art is in the Cave of El Castillo in Spain dated at about 40.8kya.[3] This art consists of a set of simple stencils of hands. Some archeologists have a controversial view that this is the work of Neanderthals.

There are about 350 caves containing more elaborate art created during prehistoric times in France and Spain.[4] The amazing thing is that the paintings began about 30kya and then spread throughout France, and Spain. Cave art has also been found in Asia, Africa and Australia and must have developed independently. While there are numerous caves in Germany, there is no cave art. The cave painting in Europe stopped about 10kya. A Google search of *European cave art* provides color examples of this beautiful art. A discussion of select caves follows:

- Chauvet Cave in France is the oldest cave with paintings of animals. The art is dated to about 32kya and was discovered in1994.[5]

---

[3] Than, Ker. 2102.
http://news.nationalgeographic.com/news/2012/06/120614-neanderthal-cave-paintings-spain-science-pike/. [Accessed: 7 Mar 2014].
[4] Curtis, Gregory, 2006, The Cave Painters, NY. Anchor Books.
[5] http://en.wikipedia.org/wiki/Chauvet_Cave. [Accessed: 7 Mar 2014].

- Font-de-Gaume is a cave in south-west France and contains more than 200 images dating back to 17kya. It was discovered in 1901.[6]
- Grotte de Cussac is a cave in France and contains about 150 works of art. It was discovered in 2000 and is estimated to be 25,000 years old. This is one of the few caves that also include human remains.[7]
- Cave of Altamira, a cave in Spain, was discovered in 1880 and was the first cave where paintings were discovered. The artwork was done between 16.5kya and 14kya. One of the most famous paintings is a vivid painting of a bison. When first discovered, there was much controversy with some believing that prehistoric man did not have the intellect to create such art.[8]

Summary of European Art

The art of *Homo sapiens* created between 30kya and 10kya is truly a wonder and is indeed true art, even by today's standard. This is the first evidence of a higher level of consciousness than had been expressed before. When one first observes the art, the thought is they had achieved full consciousness and that this is the moment in time we are seeking. But is it?

---

[6] http://en.wikipedia.org/wiki/Font-de-Gaume. [Accessed: 7 Mar 2014].
[7] http://en.wikipedia.org/wiki/Grotte_de_Cussac. [Accessed: 7 Mar 14].
[8] http://en.wikipedia.org/wiki/Cave_of_Altamira. [Accessed: 7 Mar 14].

The cave paintings leave a very strong suggestion these works were created by creative creatures with a high level of consciousness. While all of the artists were not masters, many were, as demonstrated by the proportion, balance and overall composition of their work. The figures painted consisted mainly a variety of animals such as horses, bison, lions, and cave bears. However, there are some unexpected results for art done by a creature with limited consciousness. The list of results includes:[9]

- The cave painting remained much the same for the full 20,000 years of activity. This includes the techniques and subjects for both the era and place. There were some changes over the period, but they were very subtle.

- There was a strict consistency in what was not painted: Fish are rare, insects are not present, rodents, reptiles, and birds are also absent. In each of the above subjects, they were very common in the environment.

- None of the animals are shown in landscapes. There are no trees, bushes, flowers, rivers, lakes rocks or caves. And fawns or other young are very rare.

- The colors remained very consistent also. While the artist had a wide range of colors, they typically used black and an occasional red.

---

[9] Curtis, Gregory. 2006. The Cave Painters. NY: Anchor Books.

- While a few human figures are present, they were not done with the care given to animals. The images are more like stick figures or cartoon like.

Art in Rest of World

While the European art was the most advanced, art appeared in other regions in the world at about the same time or slightly later. For example, simple art such as hand stencils dating back to 39kya were found in Indonesia.[10]

It is clear that consciousness was present, at least to a small degree, with the early innovators of this period, primarily in Europe, but throughout the world.

Conclusion on European Art

The European Art period was about 30,000 years long ranging from about 40kya to 10kya. While the art itself was magnificent, especially since it was created by prehistoric people, I believe the more significant fact is the consistency of behavior during this long period. Therefore, I include this period in the analysis, because of this special human behavior of reluctance to change for a very long time. I believe this behavior gives insight into the overall nature of humans of the early periods and to some extent the nature of humans today. We see this attribute of adversity to change present in both the Venus figures and the cave paintings.

---

[10] Bower, Bruce. 2014. Asian Cave Art Got an Early Start *Science News*. 12/27/2014. p.23.

How could such consistency of behavior for such a long time been possible? What is the answer to this mystery?

While the initial art requires some level of creativity and consciousness, I do not believe the longevity can be explained by conscious decisions. The creativity within consciousness would have surely resulted in more change. Subconscious behavior can be ruled out also, since it is derived from conscious thought. Instinct typically has the property of consistency, but it is not a learned attribute, as this must have been. Habit can also be ruled out as it is the result of repeated conscious activity that becomes automatic.

It has been suggested that this consistency was the result of training new artists to an acceptable style, which they had to conform.[11] This would require a discipline never realized at any point in human history, before or after. Even if training did explain how the art was so consistent, it does not explain the motivation to never change. Also, there is no evidence of practice or student paintings.

Furthermore, the numbers do not add up. For discussion purposes, assume a specific clan and their ancestors were responsible for a given cave and its art. For a typical cave with 200 works of art would mean a new piece of art was created every 100 years on average during the 20,000 year period of cave art. That would mean there would be many years (greater than the human life expectancy) that no art would be produced. Also, it is likely many artists would have created multiple paintings, causing even bigger

---

[11] Curtis, Gregory. 2006. *The Cave Painters*. NY: Anchor Books.

gaps in time in which art was not produced. There would be large gaps in time such that a teacher and student could not have lived at the same time.

You can play with numbers and get a similar scenario. For example, I believe it is fair to assume painting is a rare skill and is likely to be absent from time-to-time in the small clans. If the clan size was typically 20 people, and only one percent was the innovator, artist types, they would only occur once every 100 years, which is in close agreement with the number based on 200 paintings per cave.

So, another mystery emerges: How did a new innovator-artist know how to paint the next image? This is the same question of how was the knowledge of painting transferred to other caves. Since the style was a copy of previous paintings, the task was to only copy the technique rather than having to create it from scratch. I believe copying the earlier paintings was possible just as it is today. You can buy copies of many of the works of the masters with their various techniques, and they are very close. The artists who make these paintings today make no claim of being an original, and they do not have the creative talent of the master, but you end with a close approximation of the original work at a reasonable price. So it appears that after the original paintings appeared, the style and subject were locked, and the rest were copies with minor variations. This is unusual since artists typically are noted for their creativity, new ideas and change. Here we have just the opposite. I can only surmise how this art came about with these attributes.

That leaves belief as the reason for the consistency of the European art. This does make some sense if you consider that the Jewish religion has existed based on belief, for a period of about 4,000 years, in a time of high human consciousness, where change was somewhat common; compared to the cave art period, where humans were still instinctive and change was not common. Belief is also reasonable considering this is a stretch from 4,000 years (and still going) to 20,000 years.

Given that belief is the answer for the longevity of behavior, a new question arises: How did such a new belief ever originate in a society of no change? I can visualize a series of events that could have led to the first painting being accepted and then an ensuing belief that things should not change.

Consider this possible scenario. Assume an innovator creates a beautiful, full color painting of a bison on a cave wall, and assume this was right before a very successful hunt. Now, stop and think how we see images all the time in our lives; they are everywhere. And yet when we see a beautiful painting, we are often moved. Now, consider the impact the first cave painting of a bison must have had on the clan members. They had never, ever seen an image of any kind, and they surely must have been overwhelmed. It is easy to see how they might have come to believe the successful hunt was due to the image of the bison. That might have led to the beginning of a belief that this should be repeated with the other animals they hunted. A reverence must have developed for the animal in the image. It is important to view the reverence was for the animal in the image and not the painting itself. They very likely did not create art for art's sake.

With time, images of the other animals they hunted, the horse and the cave bear, were created. With the people's reluctance to change once the belief began, what was there to change it? To paint anything other than the animals at the heart of their existence was against the belief; although other subjects were occasionally created, probably by rebel innovators.

Now, I have created a story of how the cave paintings might have originated and lasted for so long. While it fits the evidence available, we do not have enough for it to be beyond conjecture. The point is that it has been shown that a reasonable story can fit the evidence we do have. Furthermore, the actual story of the origin of modern humans is not dependent on the actual story of the cave art.

The key evidence to emerge from the cave art period includes:

- Humans of that period had established a group behavior that had an extremely strong reluctance to change. We see this reluctance to change in many people living today.

- The creativity portion of their consciousness was demonstrated in the cave art; however, their consciousness was restricted to the narrow area of art, and they did not yet have full consciousness.

- The lack of full consciousness is supported by the lack of evidence for substantial population growth, and as we shall see in the next chapter that is required for survival.

I believe the key fact that emerges out of the European art period is that once a belief was established, the people were strongly opposed to change. This long period of 20ky in European cave art is the longest known period of an ongoing activity in human history without change.

Göbekli Tepe

Six miles from the ancient city of Urfa in southeastern Turkey stands possibly the most important archeological site of recent times. The site is Göbekli Tepe, and its importance is due to the fact that it upsets long-held beliefs of where and how civilization first began. Göbekli Tepe dates back to 11.6 kya or 7 millennia before the pyramids of Egypt; before writing, metal and pottery, and before the invention of the wheel.[12,13] The site consist of a series of rings encircled by massive carved limestone pillars cut and shaped with bas-relief figures of gazelles, lions, foxes, scorpions, snakes and wild boar. The largest of these stone pillars stands 18 feet tall and weighs 16 tons. There are terrazzo-like floors and graves below the floors. We not only

---

[12] Ngm.nationalgeographic.com/print/2011/06/gobekli-tepe/mann-text.
[13] http://www.smithsonianmag.com/history/gobekli-tepe-the-worlds-first-temple-83613665/?all.

have the mystery of how these stone pillars were formed, but we also see art and symbology in the figures on the pillars.

The mystery is these structures were constructed by a rather large group of hunter-gatherers who apparently settled down and lived on wild grains and other food in the area. This upsets the story of the beginning of civilization described by V. Gordon Childe as the Neolithic Revolution. Göbekli Tepe began about 1ky before the activities of the Neolithic period.

Göbekli Tepe was first examined by the German archeologist, Klaus Schmidt, in 1994 and work continues to this day. The first thing Schmidt saw was the tops of some of the pillars, which looked like grave stones, due to the fact that the site was mostly covered by the original occupants in around 8000 BC. The covering up resulted in a belly-shaped hill and that is what the name means in Turkish. Only by excavating did they realize the extent of the site.

It is generally accepted that Göbekli Tepe was a site for ritual activities and was essentially the first demonstration of religion. The people did not live at this site but rather at nearby regions. I should point out that while Göbekli Tepe is the oldest discovered so far, there are other similar, extremely old sites in the Fertile Crescent.[14]

What happened to these early people is not known. Possibly the land became depleted and could not support the population. Another possibility is that with the new sedentary lifestyle, the population increased beyond the

---

[14] www.philipcoppens.com/gobekli.html.

capability of the land to support it. This combined with the cyclic nature of good and bad crops, there may have been periods of hunger and starvation. This may have caused disenchantment with the religion to the extent they gave it up and covered the stone structures.

There is not any record of where they went or if their societies continued. Again, we have a narrow focus of religion and creativity in the art and the placement of the massive stones. All of these are signs of a higher level of consciousness, but there does not appear to be an ongoing increase in consciousness; therefore, I do not believe they reached full consciousness. There does not appear to be a significant increase in population, which appears to be necessary for continued advancements in civilization.

Conclusion on Göbekli Tepe

The discovery of Göbekli Tepe caused a major change in the thinking of how *Homo sapiens* made the transition to agriculture. Here, we had a relatively large group of hunter-gatherers who had settled down and lived on stands of wild wheat. This led to some limited increased population. Also, for the first time, we see construction of large stone structures apparently for the first sign of religious activity. The amazing fact is that these structures were constructed before the invention of the wheel, writing or any modern tools.

The key evidence we get from Göbekli Tepe includes:

- The hunter-gatherers could settle down and live on wild crops.
- Religion is observed for the first time in *Homo sapiens*.
- The ability to create the massive stone pillars with limited tools shows ingenuity associated with consciousness.
- Art and symbolism on the pillars also shows a higher level of consciousness.
- The narrowness of their activity indicates they had not yet acquired full consciousness; although, it had increased beyond the earlier hunter-gatherers.

9 THE NEOLITHIC PERIOD

We will now move into the time period where massive change was beginning to occur. I believe full consciousness does show up during this period but probably not at the beginning. I will try to better identify the moment in time when the Sapient Breakout or this change occurred and the cause for the change.

As we have seen in the previous chapter, there seemed to be a beginning of this change, with the cave art and the activities of Göbekli Tepe; however, in both cases the focus was narrow, and it appears that these societies died out and did not continue with advancement.

Change Begins

There was very little change in the behavior of *Homo sapiens* during the first 190ky. Then, around 10kya, a major change began in *Homo sapiens* behavior, first in the Fertile Crescent region of the Middle East and then later in other parts of the world. Within a short period of time, they changed from the hunter-gatherers lifestyle and began domesticating crops and animals and became farmers. This was the beginning of probably the largest change ever in human history. Populations grew, and there began an acceleration of advancements in civilization including language, literature, science, art, mathematics, metallurgy, construction, and advancement in technology that continues to this day. The small settlements became towns and cities, and the population increased dramatically. The people became more like the modern humans of today.

The transition that began about 10kya has been investigated by numerous authors for some time. The term for the transition period, Neolithic Revolution, was coined by Vere Gordon Childe in 1923 AD.[1] He described the period as the transition to agriculture, from about 10kya to the end of the prehistoric age, with the introduction of writing about 5kya. Note that I have defined the period when a human began to experience greater consciousness until the time full consciousness was realized as the Sapient Breakout. It is a shorter period of time within the Neolithic Revolution.

There are several models for the adoption of agriculture. The **Oasis** theory was proposed by Raphael Pumpelly and then popularized by Childe. This theory is based on climate conditions that caused oasis to form and forced close association of humans and animals.

There are numerous other models that theorize why the transition to agriculture occurred.[2] They include:

- **Hilly Flanks** model proposed by Robert Braidwood is where, in the hilly flanks of the Taurus and Zagros mountains in Turkey, there was fertile land and frequent rainfall that was ideal for agriculture.

---

[1] http://en.wikipedia.org/wiki/Neolithic_Revolution. [Accessed: 4 May 2013].
[2] *Ibid.*

- **Feasting** model by Brian Haden proposed that agriculture was driven by a flamboyant display of power including lavish meals, which required more food.

- **Demographic** model by Carl Sauer suggest that with an increasing sedentary population, the local wild crops were not enough to meet the needs.

Since there was no written record at this time, the actual story of the adoption of agriculture is conjecture.

Lord Colin Renfrew, a prominent British archaeologist and highly-regarded academic, was one of the principal investigators of this transition. He raised the question of why was there such a delay from the time humans migrated out of Africa, around 70kya, and the emergence of modern human behavior starting 10kya. He called this delay the **Sapient Paradox** and has done extensive study, along with others, on this question.[3,4] They believe that this transition involved both mind and culture and admit that the biological potential had to be there all along in the form of brain plasticity and a capacity for learning and communication.[5] This suggests the inherent

[3] Renfrew Colin. 1966. The sapient behavior paradox: how to test for potential? In: Mellars P, Gibson K, editors. *Modelling the early human mind. McDonald Institute.* Cambridge. UK: pp. 11–15.

[4] Renfrew, Colin. 2008. Neuroscience, evolution and the sapient paradox: the factuality of value and of the sacred. *Philosophical Transactions of the Royal Society B, Biological Sciences.* June 12, 363(1499), pp. 2041-2047.

[5] Donald, Merlin. 2009. Book Review: The sapient paradox: can cognitive neuroscience solve it? *Brain - A Journal of Neurology.* 132. pp.820-824.

presence of some level of consciousness. But, when was it was fully realized?

The original view on the sequence of events for this change was a very orderly transition of humans from hunter-gatherer to the modern-thinking human. The original sequence was believed to be:

- The Ice Age ended, making the climate more suitable for crops.
- Humans changed from hunter-gatherer to farmers and settled down.
- Crops and animals were domesticated.
- Populations increased.
- Innovation increased.

The evidence now shows this was not the exact sequence of events. First of all, we see from Göbekli Tepe that hunter-gatherers could settle down and live on wild wheat. The end of the Ice Age with the milder climate would have made wild crops more abundant.

With the settling down of the hunter-gatherer due to the abundance of wild grains, one would expect the population would increase, and the evidence shows the worldwide population did increase. And yet, these people were still hunter-gatherers.

So the obvious question is why did the people of the Fertile Crescent begin to farm? I believe the Demographic model proposed by Carl Sauer and adapted by Lewis Binford is closest to the actual events. This model says that human population is hampered by the natural environment in supplying food capacity and that with increased population the natural supplies become too insignificant.[6]

My conjecture of how farming began follows. The end of the Ice Age brought about an abundance of wild crops. With this new abundance, the clan did not have to move as often in search of food. Their length of stay at a given location lengthened, until the stay was a year. They in effect settled down full time, probably without realizing the implications. Gone was the strong deterrent of having too many children in the nomad lifestyle, where they had to carry the children and only could carry so many. They began to have more children, and that made it difficult if not impossible to go back to the nomad lifestyle. They, in effect, were trapped.

I suspect their lifestyle was a hybrid of hunting while operating out of a fixed base and gathering the nearby wild crops. At this point in time they were still hunter-gatherers. That would have been a relatively minor change from the pure hunter-gatherer lifestyle. This is important because of the strong resistance to change as observed in the people of the cave art.

With the increased population, they were trapped with making it almost impossible to go back to the pure hunter-gatherer. Now, suppose over time the wild crops

[6] Bareja, Ben G. 2011. *The History of Agriculture is Revisited.* Crop Farming Review. Available at: http://www.cropsreview.com/history-of-agriculture.html. [Accessed: 2 May 2015].

could not support the population, either due to excessive population growth and/or poor crop yield due to weather. The solution could have come from the innovators who set about to improve wild crop yield, such as clearing more land for the wild crop. These people would have had a good understanding of how crops propagate and grow – they had lived off the land for thousands of years. The next step would have been to enhance the wild crops by cultivating and planting additional crops, which then becomes farming. Over time, the next logical step would have been to domesticate animals already living in the area. We cannot be sure this is what actually happened, but the scenario does show a likely path to overcome the resistance to change. They had to make the change. It is fair to say that once this transition started, it would have been even harder to go back.

The transition from hunter-gatherer to modern humans was an evolutionary change. The change, when it began around 10kya, happened rather quickly and was very significant. One author notes that as an example, the people in the Fertile Crescent, as late as 9000 B.C., were still hunter-gatherers, but by 6000 B.C., they were totally dependent on crops and domestic animals.[7] In another report, there was evidence of humans shifting from hunting ungulates and small animals to managing sheep and goats over a short period of several hundred years around 8200 BC at a site in

---

[7] Diamond, Jared. 2005. *Guns, Germs, and Steel.* New York: W.W. Norton Company. P 142.

Turkey.[8] The point is that after a lifestyle of hunting and gathering, over the period of about 2,000,000 years for the *Homo* species, the shift to agriculture by *Homo sapiens* was made in a very short period of time. This was possible because of the attribute of consciousness present in the "new" creature, *Homo sapiens*. Given this evidence, a more accurate sequence of events in the transition to agriculture can be presented:

- The Ice Age ended.
- Because of the milder climate, an abundance of wild crops became available.
- The hunter-gatherer had less need to roam and became dependent on the wild crops.
- Lifestyle became a hybrid one of settling down, collecting from the abundant wild crops, and then hunting from the fixed home base.
- Population increased significantly making going back to the nomad lifestyle impossible.
- Out of necessity, the wild crops were enhanced making this the first steps toward agriculture.

It is believed that the reason early agriculture originated in the Fertile Crescent was due to the abundance

---

[8] http://popular-archaeology.com/issue/03012014/article/scientists-uncover-evidence-of-change-from-hunting-to-herding-at-early-neolithic-settlement. [Accessed: 30 April 2015].

of wild crops suitable for farming and animals suitable for domestication, in addition to an ideal climate. The initial crops were the *founder crops*, emmer wheat, einkorn wheat and barley, flax, pea, chickpea bitter vetch and lentil.[9] The animals first domesticated included sheep, goats, pig and the dromedary camel.[10]

Agriculture in the Rest of the World

While our focus has been on what is believed the original site of the first agriculture, the Fertile Crescent, be aware that agriculture also occurred independently in many other regions throughout the world. Since agriculture developed independently around the world at about the same time, one would expect there to be a common factor that brought it all about. The factor, most likely, was the favorable climate brought about by the end of the Ice Age.

Also, note that these times are long before writing appeared and you will find discrepancies in the dates often with overlap by different authors. The variations can be as large as 1,000 to 3,000 years. Part of the confusion also comes from the definition of the time, ranging from the very first time of occurrence to the time of establishment, such as agriculture. For comparison, it is best to stay with the same author to get a better relative time on a particular subject.

In addition, each of the transitions around the world was different because of the differences in the resources of crops and animals suitable for domestication. A summary of

---

[9] http://en.wikipedia.org/wiki/Neolithic_Revolution.
[10] Ibid.

the key independent agriculture events around the world are shown below:[11]

- 12k BC – Near East, first agriculture revolution.
- 12k BC – Levant (in Near East), domesticated wheat
- 9k BC – Egypt, wheat, barley, jujube.[12]
- 8.5k BC –Fertile Crescent, founder crops.
- 7.5k BC – China, rice, millet.[13]
- 7.5k BC – Mesoamerica, maize.
- 7k BC – Southern Europe, wheat, barley, small animals.
- 7k BC – Pakistan, wheat, sesame, barley and eggplant.
- 7k BC – Pakistan, cattle and chicken.
- 6.8k BC –Southeast Asia, rice.
- 6k BC – Pakistan, granary for storage of excess food.
- 5.5k BC –Ireland, first enclosed field system.
- 5.1k BC – North America, common squash.[14]
- 4k BC – Egypt, bread made using yeast.
- 4k BC – Mesopotamia, first use of wooden plough.
- 3.5k BC –Mesopotamia, first use of irrigation.
- 3.5k BC –Americas (Ecuador), first agriculture.

---

[11]http://en.wikipedia.org/wiki/Timeline_of_agriculture_and_food_tech nology.

[12] http://en.wikipedia.org/wiki/Neolithic_Revolution. [Accessed: 5 Feb. 2015].

[13] http://en.wikipedia.org/wiki/Agriculture_in_China. [Accessed: 6 Feb. 2015].

[14] http://anthrojournal.com/issue/october-2001/article/the-origins-and-development-of-an-indigenous-agriculture-comples-in-easter-notrh-america. [Accessed: 6 Feb. 2015]. Note this may have been wild squash.

- 3k BC – India, sugar produced.
- 2.3k BC – North America, common squash.[15]

The above is just a small sample of the activities of societies that converted from the hunter-gatherer to the farmer lifestyle, and most of these were isolated from each other; therefore, the conversion was independent. Other societies near the early converts just adopted the agriculture of their neighbors. Essentially, most all societies throughout the world made this conversion with only a few exceptions. One obvious exception is that of the Eskimo as their land is ill sited for agriculture.

Another potential exception is the aborigines of Australia. They were among the first to migrate out of Africa, first arriving in Australia between 40kya to 80kya.[16] It was long thought that these people always lived a nomadic hunter-gatherer lifestyle; however, recent research shows they farmed as an activity rather than a lifestyle.[17] They cultivated the land to emphasize the natural order of things and moved when it was advantageous. They, in effect, very effectively combined the hunter-gatherer with the farmer lifestyle. They did not build permanent dwellings as other farmers. They also did not advance much beyond that lifestyle, and that is probably the cause for the belief they

---

15 Ibid.

16 http://en.wikipedia.org/wiki/History-of-Indigenous-Australians. [Accessed: 7 Feb. 1015].

17 http://www.smh.com.au/action/printArticle?id=2661295. [Accessed: 7 Feb. 2015].

were primitive. The reason the Australian aborigines did not progress further is believed due to the limited population of only a few hundred thousand people. Compared to the tens of millions of people in the advancing regions, meant the aboriginal Australians had a limited number of innovators to create the advancements.[18] A similar situation existed in New Guinea.

Another short-term exception is the European hunter-gatherers and farmers, which coexisted for 2,000 years.[19] Humans first arrived in Europe about 45kya and then, about 7.5kya immigrant farmers brought agriculture and the sedentary lifestyle. However, not all accepted the change and remained hunter-gatherers for about 2ky. A recent study showed the northern Europeans were slow to adopt farming.[20] The interesting thing about this study is that for the first time ornaments were used to distinguish between the farmers and those retaining the hunter-gatherer lifestyle. Each had their own style of beads to distinguish their culture, either farmer or hunter-gatherer.[21]

Finally, there are isolated, small groups of people around the world in isolated areas that still live the hunter-gatherer lifestyle.

---

[18] Diamond, Jared. 2005. *Guns, Germs, and Steel.* New York: W.W. Norton Company. p 311.
[19] Bower, Bruce. 2013. Ancient Farmers, Foragers Kept Genes to Themselves. *Science News Magazine.* November 16, 2013, p13.
[20] http://phys.org/news/2015-04-dont-farm-northern-europeans-neolithic.html. [Accessed: 9 April 2015].
[21] Bower, Bruce, 2015. *Beads suggest hunter-gatherers resisted farming in Northern Europe.* Science News Magazine. May 16. 2015. p. 11

The key thing to note from this discussion is the fact that the farmer lifestyle was adopted by the vast majority of people in favor of the hunter-gatherer lifestyle, which had been that of the entire previous *Homo* genus for the previous two million years. The amazing thing is the transition for a single society was typically 3ky or less, and the independent societies throughout the whole world made the transition in about 10ky.

Population

We have seen that with the sedentary lifestyle of the early farmers, there was a major growth in population. Population in this early period is difficult to accurately determine, however numerous investigators have made estimates. During the very early years of the *Homo sapiens*, population was relatively flat. Worldwide population by 37kya is estimated at three million but then jumps to ten to fifteen million by 10kya, prior to the beginning of agriculture.[22] Another source estimates world-wide population at 10kya ranged from one million to ten million with four million being the typical number.[23] The uncertainty of the numbers is obvious. By 5kya, when agriculture had become well established, the population estimate ranges from five million to twenty million. This represents

---

[22] Hoggan, Ron, 2010, Life Expectancy in the Paleolithic, Available at: htpp://paleodiet.com/life-expectancy.htm. [Accessed: 14 February 2014].

[23] http://www.census.gov/population/international/data/worldpop/table_history.php.

population growth of 2x to 5x. I believe the 5x number is more accurate.

These estimates show the population growth began prior to the adoption of agriculture and supports the view that the clans did settle down and lived on wild crops. The population could not have increased as it did if the hunter-gatherer clans were still on the move. It is also easy to see how population growth would outstrip the capability of wild crops to supply adequate food.

With the population growth, there also was growth in the number of innovators, and that is what fueled even more population with advances in agriculture and then later advances in other fields of civilization. It is fair to say that population growth was necessary for growth of civilization.

The three groups of people, from the cave art, Göbekli Tepe and the Fertile Crescent agriculture, all had in common an initial narrow focus utilizing limited consciousness. However, those focusing on agriculture led to a continuation of their society because their focus led to increased population and more innovators who expanded the focus allowing for a broader enhancement of civilization. This is what was missing from the Cave Art and the Göbekli Tepe period.

Agriculture – Good or Bad?

Although the shift to agriculture from the hunter-gatherer lifestyle is generally believed to have been a good move that opinion is not shared by all. Agriculture brought about changes in human lifestyle that allowed for our modern society to develop. With the ability to produce excess food and then store it, time was freed up for other activities. A separation of labor developed, and new fields of endeavor emerged over time, including writing, language, literature, arts, mathematics, science, technology, social change, and the information society we are now in. However, many horrific wars also followed along with other evils committed by some groups against others.

In addition to these disadvantages, agriculture brought about other negatives. Jared Diamond is one who thinks the move to agriculture was the worst mistake in the history of the human race.[24] He cited three reasons to believe agriculture is bad for health:

- Hunter-gatherers enjoyed a varied diet, while the food of farmers was from a few starchy crops.
- Dependence on a limited number of crops put them at risk if a crop failed.
- Agriculture brought about population increase, and that led to crowding and increased disease.

Diamond makes the statement, "Forced to choose between limiting population or trying to increase food production, we chose the latter and ended up with starvation, warfare, and tyranny."[25]

While there is some truth to Diamond's view, agriculture brought about advances in civilization that would

---

[24] http://www.ditext.com/diamond/mistake.htm. [Accessed: 7 February 2015]
[25] *Ibid.*

not have been possible otherwise. I also question if full consciousness could have been fully realized without the agriculture revolution and the advances that followed. Full consciousness is a lot like free will. Both provide the opportunity to do great good, but with them, you also have the possibility of horrific results. Possibly, the problem is not agriculture but the acquisition of full consciousness. Whatever the case, you and I would not be here today, and you would not be reading this book. There would be no books to read. There would not be the civilization we have today. Maybe by limiting the population, as with the hunter-gatherer lifestyle, we could have maintained the innocence of a simple lifestyle - or maybe not.

Conclusions of the Neolithic Period

In the Neolithic period starting about 10kya, there is the beginning of massive changes in the behavior of *Homo sapiens*. It begins with the end of the Ice Age with the climate becoming much milder and more conducive to plant growth. We see the hunter-gatherers move toward becoming farmers. Because of the reluctance to change, this was not a conscious change. I believe it was more of an accident rather than a planned move. The model for the conversion to agriculture was universal and worked for all the independent regions of the world where the change to agriculture occurred. There had to be a common trigger that initiated the process, and I believe that had to be the climate, and specifically, the moderation of the weather due to the ending of the Ice Age.

By the time farming started, the population had grown significantly. Up to this point, there had not been a need for widespread full consciousness, although, I believe with increased population, there was pressure for enhancement of farming and the need for some increase in consciousness.

The key evidence we get from the Neolithic Period follows:

- With the end of the Ice Age, wild crops grew in abundance, reducing the need for movement of the hunter-gatherers.

- Eventually the hunter-gatherers settled down, and population increased significantly, preventing the return to the nomad lifestyle, causing the need for early farming.

- As population increased, the number of innovators increased, and that was necessary to satisfy the need for increased consciousness to cope with the pressures of increased population.

- I believe it is profound that *Homo sapiens* after being on Earth for nearly 200,000 years, the major transition to agriculture occurred independently throughout the world in less than 10,000 years.

.

10 THE MODERN PERIOD

As agriculture became established, free time increased, and some activity turned to other endeavors. We see a rapid development of new capabilities never before seen by any other living creature. These rapid changes suggest consciousness was becoming more common, where in earlier times, it only appeared in a very limited degree and in occasional periods of time, usually disconnected from prior times. There now appears to be a continuum of consciousness from one period to the next. To some it might appear that consciousness was evolving; instead it was becoming less suppressed as it moved toward full consciousness. Had full consciousness been realized, or was it still emerging during this period? The advancements provide an answer. A summary of advancements in the period immediately following the agriculture revolution, up until the founding of Rome is shown in the following list:[1]

- 24k BC – First pottery – China
- 4.7k BC – First pyramid (Djoser) - Egypt

---

[1] This summary is compiled from commonly known data and various sources on the internet. Also, note that the dates will vary depending on the source and the definition of the event. The data is not representative as being exact but rather to show the relative short time in which these advancements occurred..

- 4.5k BC – First copper smelting – Middle East
- 4.5 BC –   First city - Mesopotamia
- 3.5k BC – Wheel – Mesopotamia
- 3.5k BC – Potter's wheel – Middle East
- 3.3k BC – First writing, cuneiform – Mesopotamia
- 3k BC –   First bronze – Turkey, Mesopotamia
- 1.3k BC –Iron age beginning – Middle E & SE Europe
- 753 BC –   Rome Founded – Italy

Note the time first pottery predates the time of the first agriculture; therefore, it was made by hunter-gatherers. It is not hard to imagine this might have occurred. A person playing with clay, a common substance, drops it into the fire and notices later that it changed and is now very hard – the first pottery. This is probably how some of the first Venus figures were made. Many years later, the process of making pottery objects was refined.

One thing that does stand out is the large number of developments made in the Middle East – hence, the name the Cradle of Civilization. It is also interesting to note that many developments were often made independently at other isolated locations.

The key evidence we get from the Modern Period follows:

- With the advances made during this period, it is obvious the mental abilities were well beyond those of the early hunter-gatherers, and increased consciousness was required for at least a significant portion of the population. The question remains as to how many people were required to have full consciousness.

- The Sapient Breakout began rather early in the beginning of agriculture. However, full consciousness was not required in the beginning, based on the above discussion. Keep in mind we see a difference in dates as large as 3,000 years, depending on the author and their definition of the event. I would choose a date of about 8000 B.C. as the beginning of the Sapient Breakout based on the estimates by Jared Diamond.[2] I believe his projections of time are more accurate than most other sources.

- While consciousness did grow with advancements in agriculture, it still did not require full consciousness because of the narrow scope of agriculture. As humans moved into other areas the need for consciousness increased. It did continue to grow, and I believe that by early in the Modern Period full consciousness was present in essentially all people.

This would place the Sapient Breakout Period from 8000 BC to 4000 BC with full consciousness present at the end of the period or about 4000 BC.

---

[2] Diamond, Jared. 2005. *Guns, Germs, and Steel.* New York: W.W. Norton Company. p 142.

During this time, we see innovators first to expand the scope of consciousness, then the realization of consciousness by other members of the clan and finally, we see full consciousness in all people as we see today.

However, keep in mind that this is just an estimate on my part.

11 CONSCIOUSNESS SUPPRESSED

The concept of how consciousness emerged is a bit farfetched and not what you normally see in nature. To have consciousness be present, but not be detectable, is counterintuitive. However, the argument that consciousness must have been present in the first *Homo sapiens* is based on solid logic using the principal of Non-Evolving Attributes, and that is very strong evidence. Consciousness just appeared in the early *Homo sapiens* without any natural explanation. It clearly was a supernatural event. While the early *Homo sapiens* clearly had the attribute of consciousness, their behavior was essentially the same as their predecessor species, and any sign of consciousness was very weak. The evidence presented to date is the early humans acted just as you would expect an instinctive creature to do. Because the concept that consciousness was suppressed in early humans is so important to the overall story, I want to share additional evidence to support the concept.

Small Number of Innovations

One factor supporting the view that consciousness was suppressed in early humans is the small number of advancements or inventions compared to the modern human. One might argue that it is best explained by the population values, before and after. Early on, the population was very low, and the number of innovators was also very low; at times there were no innovators present in the clans. And since it is believed that all advancements were made by innovators, one would expect a very low rate of new advancements. However, there is a subtle point here that should be pointed out. Even though the rate of new innovations is low, it does suggest that consciousness was present at a low level and, on occasion, it showed up in some advancements, and that the rate of innovations was probably higher than in previous *Homo* species.

While I do believe that the low innovator population density was a contributing favor in the advancement rate, I do not believe it is the whole story.

Creation Stories

There is strong motivation for everyone to know where they came from, and essentially every society on Earth today has their own story of how they came about – their creation story. Apparently, it is the nature of humans to want to know how they came into being. That is what this book is about on a large scale. Since most of the stories were the result of imagination, we find they are all different, although there are many common elements. It was common to dismiss creation stories of other people as myths, since the law of noncontradiction says they all cannot be true.

There are different categories of creation stories, including:[1]

- Creation from chaos
- Earth diver
- Emergence
- *Ex nihilo* (out of nothing)
- World parent

They are also commonly categorized by regions. While each creation myth is unique, there often is some common characteristic. One of the most common is the existence of a supreme being or god.

The number of stories collected by various authors is numerous. There is a list of 100 creation myths on Wilkipedia.[2] In the book by Barbara Sproul, 136 myths are listed, and she admits the list is only partial.[3]

I believe the most profound fact about the creation stories is that each society believes they were created right where they were at the time, and none mentions or has any recall of having walked thousands of miles to reach their current location. There is nothing in their memory about that experience. That tells me that they migrated to their location before their consciousness was expressed. And that the stories must have been created by their imaginations long

---

[1] http://en.wilipedia.org/wiki/List_of_creation_myths. [Accessed: 17 February 2015].

[2] Ibid.

[3] Sproul, Barbara. 1979. *Primal Myths, Creation Myths Around the World*, NY Harper One.

after they arrived at their current location. There is one other possibility, but it can only be true for one story. That story is that the truth of their creation was revealed to them by God as in the Jewish religion.

The fact that there is no recall of the long walk makes it clear that at the time of their walk, they did yet have full consciousness and were still basically in the instinctive mode. Consciousness was still suppressed to a large extent.

Religion

It is important to note that to have a sense of a god or a supreme spiritual being requires consciousness. You have to think about such a thing. The first sign of religion among humans was first observed at Göbekli Tepe. While these people were still gather-hunters, they were showing limited signs of having consciousness, at least in a spiritual mode. In all the archeological artifacts from previous people, there is no sign of any god or religious evidence. This is key since after consciousness was acquired, essentially every society has some sense of a god. It is fundamental to the nature of humans after they acquired consciousness.

This profound fact tells me that to experience a god or religion requires consciousness, and therefore consciousness prior to Göbekli Tepe was suppressed.

War

There is one other factor that may support the idea that consciousness was suppressed in early *Homo sapiens.* When we look at animals, we see instinctive behavior and not evil. When a lion kills a gazelle, it is a natural act to acquire food and is not considered an evil act. In the religious sense, an instinctive creature does not sin. Evil or sin can only come about with a human with consciousness that makes decisions to do harm. Research has shown that war originated only within the past 10,000 years and was not present in early instinctive humans. This supports the view that consciousness was suppress initially.[4]

I would point out that not all agree with the conclusions of this report. It is possible that any exceptions to the low aggression might be due to some low level of consciousness.

These factors: small number of innovations, creation stories, religion and lack of wars, support the idea that consciousness was suppressed initially and was present only in a limited amount.

Purpose of Suppression of Consciousness

One obvious question is: What is the purpose of suppressing consciousness until a later date? Why not just have it be present as *Homo sapiens* were introduced 200kya? I believe there is a very good answer. It seems obvious that God wanted the whole Earth populated with humans. That had not been done before; none of the earlier *Homo* species made it to the Americas. Now, look at the difference between the early, instinctive humans versus those with full consciousness. The instinctive creature, like animals, did not

---

[4] Bower, Bruce. 2013. War Arose Recently, Analysis Claims. *Science News*, 8/13/2013, p.10

kill unnecessarily or cause conflict. However, the fully consciousness humans with free will often make evil choices and war with other humans.[5] The fully consciousness primitive humans have demonstrated excessive violence. For example, today in New Guinea, where you have fully conscious, but primitive humans, who have an encounter with another unfamiliar native, they will engage in a long discussion to determine if they are kin. If they determine they are not relatives they will try to kill each other.[6]

I believe humans with full consciousness would have engaged in conflict with their neighbors, and as a result of this distraction they would not have migrated at the same rate as the instinctive creatures. They likely would not have ever populated the entire world because of the conflict caused by war. So, the initial suppression of consciousness was part of God's necessary plan to have the whole Earth populated by humans.

Conclusion

With these four arguments for suppression of consciousness in early humans combined with their early behavior as instinctive driven creatures, we have strong evidence of the truth of the story as presented. Combine this with the fact that consciousness universally appeared worldwide among isolated societies in a short period of time,

---

[5] Bower, Bruce, 2013, War Arose Recently, Analysis Claims, *Science News*, 8/13/2013, p.10

[6] Diamond, Jared. 2005. *Guns, Germs, and Steel*. New York: W.W. Norton Company. p 272.

and the fact that we have strong evidence that consciousness must have already been present but was just not yet expressed.

12 CONSCIOUSNESS EXPRESSED

With the fact of consciousness suppression in early humans clearly established, we will now look at how the process was reversed and consciousness became expressed. This event is what I defined earlier as the Sapient Breakout. While the suppression of consciousness was a supernatural event that occurred at the time *Homo* sapiens first appeared, I believe expression was a natural event. The realization or expression of consciousness occurred over a period of time at independent locations all around the world. This makes the process much more complicated. One reason is that there are many unanswered questions.

For example, it appears that consciousness was available in a limited degree to various individuals, innovators, over the course of history? Was this low level of consciousness available to all or just a select few? Was the consciousness available continuously to these individuals or did it just appear at select times? And if it did appear at select times, was there some trigger that brought it about? Also, was the full spectrum of consciousness available or were just select components of consciousness available?

There are three possible scenarios that would explain how consciousness was expressed.

Divine Intervention

Since it appears that the suppression of consciousness was a supernatural event; and therefore, an act of God, you might assume the same would be true for the release of the suppression or the expression of consciousness. I believe this unlikely for the reason that I see God acting more efficiently, and therefore He probably would have created a process to achieve the result without His direct intervention. Therefore, I do not see this has a likely scenario.

Epigenetics

Our consciousness, once expressed, is a stable and rock-solid attribute of humans. Therefore, it is possible that it is encoded in our DNA. Our DNA cannot be switched on or off directly, but it can be controlled by epigenetics, in which the gene function is altered without altering the DNA. Typically, a part of the DNA, once thought to be junk DNA, sits on top (therefore the name epi) of a region of the DNA and changes the gene function of that part of the DNA. It can be affected by the environment and is heritable. The key question is: Does an epigenetic control have the capability to last for 200,000 years? Assuming it does, epigenetics appears to be a candidate for the process we are looking for. Epigenetics is an exciting new field of biology and many developments are occurring rapidly. For this author to research this field adequately to address our problem at hand would be both inefficient and ineffective. Therefore, I will leave it experts to later determine if epigenetics is the answer and specifically how it might work. However, I believe there is a more plausible explanation.

Practice Makes Perfect

The third and I believe a likely scenario for how consciousness was transformed from being suppressed is somewhat vague and a bit hard to describe. Suppose the early humans had the capability of consciousness but did not realize they had it. We have all heard the statement: "Use it or lose it." as it applies to the brain. I believe there must be a corollary statement: "Use it and gain it." How many times have you started a new activity, and realized you had a talent you did not know you had? Could consciousness be like this?

Thinking or deep thinking, as in consciousness, must have been a totally out-of-the-box activity with early humans and probably not very well received by other members of the clan. It probably would have been like the ten year old sitting in class, looking out the window and daydreaming instead of doing his studies. Such an activity would not be readily accepted by the clan. Their primary thoughts must have been in obtaining food and what value is this thing, thinking that you are doing? Could the social pressure against using consciousness been strong enough to suppress it for nearly 200ky? Actually, it did not totally suppress it. As we have seen earlier, the advancements were made by the rare innovator who only appeared in an occasional generation.

Keep in mind that the bulk of this time the world was in a major Ice Age and times were especially hard. Then when the Ice Age ended, the climate moderated, life became easier and there was something new, leisure time. It is then when we see results of more incidents of consciousness with the cave art, Göbekli Tepe and the beginning of agriculture in the Fertile Crescent. Furthermore, in each of these examples we still only see a small portion of consciousness. We do see the randomness of creativity discussed earlier – art in one case, religion and the idea to arrange massive stones in a pattern in another and ideas on how to improve crop yield in another.

In none of these cases do we see full consciousness. And when you review the long list of consciousness attributes discussed earlier, you realize that while you have the basic capabilities, it may take many years of experience to realize the benefits of full consciousness. That is why I now believe the Sapient Breakout occurred over a period of many years in which the societies began to develop and utilize their inherent capability of consciousness.

Agriculture Dominates

Of the three cases discussed where we see signs of limited consciousness, only agriculture had several long term benefits. The first was it provided food for the survival of the clan. That was an ongoing need of the society. Neither the cave art nor the activities at Göbekli Tepe provided this. In addition, population growth was another benefit that allowed agriculture to continue and flourish. That was not the case for the other two, and as a result, they apparently died out.

The primary driver for the beginning of agriculture was the improved climate and that was the reason for the worldwide adoption of agriculture. Once agriculture started, it continued to grow and that allowed attention to be turned to the next set of advancements. It truly was the beginning of civilization. We see the first signs of division of labor that then provided for additional growth.

Surely, the early recipients of consciousness were the innovators, but their level of consciousness was not the full spectrum. Next, I believe we see four things happen over time:

- As population increased, those around the innovators, the leaders, friends and others also begin to experience consciousness. Consciousness must have a contagious property. Instead of only a lone innovator having consciousness, there was now a group with the capability and that promoted the further growth of consciousness.

- With continuing increases in population, there was an unending need to improve the agriculture and that drove new innovation, keeping the need for increased consciousness.

- The consciousness expressed might have been heritable, but there is no evidence available. A stronger factor might have been the children growing up in an atmosphere of consciousness would have easily adopted it also.

- As the population grew and societies became larger, the scope of problems expanded, and the need of consciousness would have also expanded.

As stated in the previous chapter, I believe the Sapient Breakout Period was from 8000 BC to 4000 BC with full consciousness expressed at the end of the period.

13 COMPLETE HUMANS

As some might expect, the evidence presented here in many cases points uniquely to a spiritual explanation, based on the principal of following the evidence wherever it leads. As I pointed out in the beginning, I wanted this analysis to be done in a secular manner, so that those without spiritual beliefs would follow the evidence presented and then in the end, they could draw their own conclusions. We have seen some early evidence of the spiritual in the previous two chapters, and now, we will see an even stronger influence in the story. I wonder, as we complete the story, if the evidence for the supernatural is now so strong that the secular person might consider an objective reexamination of their beliefs? It is just a thought worth considering.

I believe the spiritual implications are very strong, and this analysis would not be complete without their consideration. Keep in mind that this is simply the result of following the evidence wherever it leads. It now seems to me that a complete, reasonable, and logical explanation is difficult, if not impossible, without the spiritual component. I was an atheist for many years before I took an objective look at the evidence for the existence of God, realized I had been wrong all those years, and then accepted Christ. However, be aware that I have the utmost respect for your views, whatever they may be. I am interested in your conclusions, either in the spiritual realm or not. If you desire, my website is listed following the cover page and is available for comments.

The only area where my religious beliefs have any influence on the conclusions is the simple belief that if God is theistic[1], as I believe He is, then He is involved with events of the universe, either by bringing them about by natural means that we could not detect, or by supernatural means that should be obvious to us. Furthermore, we should expect to see evidence of His involvement in key important events in the creation and operation of the universe. You would expect to see God's involvement in the key events such as the creation of the universe, the creation of life on Earth and the creation of humans on Earth, and that is exactly what the evidence shows.

Homo sapiens

Next, we will look at the story of *Homo sapiens*. About 200kya, *Homo sapiens* first appeared on Earth. They, in many respects, were similar to their predecessor, *Homo* species ancestors, except they were the most advanced to date.

We know from Chapter 5, and the principle of NEA that the early *Homo sapiens* had consciousness, although it was suppressed. The question is: Was this new attribute just added to the most recent of the *Homo* creatures that had evolved up to that point, or did God introduce a totally new creature, *Homo sapiens*, which were more streamlined and

---

[1] theism – The belief in a single personal God who created and is the ruler of the universe.

anatomically advanced to introduce theses new attributes? There is evidence that *Homo sapiens* were a new creature that appeared very suddenly in what is described as the "big bang of human evolution".[2] Paleoanthropologists, Dennell and Roebroeks stated the human-like fossils appear so suddenly in the archeological record that "it is hard at present to identify its immediate ancestry in east Africa. Not for nothing has it been described as a hominin 'without an ancestor, without a clear past.'"[3,4] The most reasonable answer to the question is that *Homo sapiens* are totally new creatures, created and placed on Earth by God in a supernatural event. This would fit with the concept that we have a totally new set of attributes being added at that same time.

This event is so similar to the origin-of-life event, as discussed in Appendix B, so you might wonder if someone is likely to say this also is panspermia.[5] This is obviously not the case; therefore, if this event is not due to panspermia, then, it is reasonable to believe neither is the origin-of-life event.

---

[2] University of Michigan. News and information Services News Release. "New study suggests big bang theory of human evolution" (January 10, 2000). Available at:

http://www.umich.edu/~newsinfo/Releases/2000/Jan00/r01100b.html.

[3] Robin Dennell and Wil Roebroeks. "An Asian perspective on early human dispersal from Africa." *Nature*. Vol. 438:1099-1104. (Dec22/29, 2005).

[4] http://www.evolutionnews.org/2008/01/the_facts_about_intelligent_de004737.html.

[5] Panspermia is the theory that life on Earth originated in outer space and was seeded here by various means. See discussion in Appendix B.

The *Homo sapiens* are so advanced compared to any of the previous *Homo* species; they cannot be explained by Darwinian Evolution. Maybe instead, it was evolution of design, and as stated earlier, maybe the earlier *Homo* creatures were prototypes, design prototypes in God's design of *Homo sapiens*. If God did not design *Homo sapiens* as a new creature that did not evolve, then what was the purpose of the previous *Homo* species other than design prototypes? This is a somewhat radical concept, even for believers. I accept that this statement may upset some believers because of their belief that God is omniscient, all knowing; and therefore, did not need prototypes to know how to create humans. I do strongly believe God is omniscient and does know everything that is knowable. However, if knowledge is infinite, as I believe it is, then, God's knowledge is also infinite. And, what does infinite mean other than ever increasing? It is this increasing knowledge that is God's ongoing learning that supports my belief that God is a dynamic God, as does at least one other author, Gerald Schroeder.[6] And, part of God's increased knowledge is gained from the earlier *Homo* prototypes. This model does provide a reason for the existence of the earlier *Homo* creatures that is not Darwinian Evolution.

In the final analysis, I believe it is reasonable to believe that *Homo sapiens* are a special type, created by God in a supernatural event and not just an advanced degree of previous creatures.

---

[6] Schroeder, Gerald. 2009. *GOD, According to God*, NY: Harper Collins.

Additional Unique Human Attributes

Are humans complete with the addition of consciousness, or are there other attributes that add to the completeness of humans? Again, examining humans today for common attributes, we find four more that uniquely fit the NEA criteria. While not as strong at the consciousness attribute, all of these attributes are universal with essentially all people on Earth, even though they are separated by thousands of miles. These attributes are:

- Moral code
- Conscience
- Concept of a god
- Free Will

Using the principle of NEA, we can say that each of these attributes was acquired at the same time as consciousness, at the introduction of *Homo sapiens,* just like consciousness was acquired. Since each of these attributes requires consciousness to be realized, and since consciousness is initially suppressed, they were in effect, also suppressed; therefore, we do not see evidence of these attributes in the early *Homo sapiens.*

We will now look at each one of these attributes individually, and then see how they are uniquely related.

Moral Code – Evidence shows that an objective moral code is present in all humans; however, it is marginally strong, and it may be modified, either weakened or strengthened, by their culture, either by traditions or ideology. The best example of the moral code is the universal golden rule, which says: "Do unto others as you would have them do unto you." This rule, in various forms, is present in essentially all religions and cultures.[7]

Evidence of an objective moral code is supported by results from tests run with infants less than a year old.[8] The infants were shown a puppet show where a central character puppet was trying to climb a steep hill. Another helper puppet was trying to aid the climber, while a hinderer puppet was trying to stop the climber. Later, the infants were shown both the helper and the hinderer puppet and encouraged to reach for one. Almost all favored the helper puppet and rejected the hinderer puppet, clearly showing the ability of the infants to know right from wrong. Paul Bloom, one of the investigators with puppets, indicates that babies come with hard-wired moral universals.[9] I agree with that.

How do very small children know what is right and wrong, good and bad? They, at a young age, have not yet been taught what is good or bad. Obviously, it is not by knowing rules in a formal, leather-bound book. However, I believe that a child can know when an act hurts or helps another person or the surroundings, the environment, and

---

[7] Hht://www.huffingtonpoist.com/donna-henes/golden-rule_b_202245.html?view=print&comm._ref=false. [Accessed: 2 February 2014].

[8] http://www.nature.com/news/2007/071121/full/news.2007.278.html. [Accessed: 2/9/2015].

[9] Cook, Gareth. 2013. The Moral Life of Babies, by Paul Bloom. *Scientific American*. 11/12/2013, Available at: http://www.scientificamerican.com/article/the-moral-life0of-babies/?print=true. [Accessed: 22 February 2014].

that is what determines what is right and what is wrong. I believe it is that simple.

With adults, the knowledge of right and wrong becomes more sophisticated, but it is still inherent in the makeup of the person. As they grow older, humans are taught the rules of their society, and that may modify some of their inherent moral rules; either to enhance or degrade them.

Some people have come to believe in a relativistic view of morality, rather than in objective moral values.[10] This view of morality, moral relativism, states morality is determined by the standard of a person's own authorities. In other words, morality is whatever an individual decides. But, is that correct, and are there no absolutes in morality?

Another view stated by Bloom in his book indicates that these moral foundations are the products of biological evolution.[11] Most naturalists believe morals evolved, but that also has some problems as evolution is a selfish process, and that is contrary to the values in the moral code. That issue is best questioned by Thomas Nagel in his book, *Mind and Cosmos*, which was reviewed by Brian Leiter.[12] Nagel asks: "If our moral facilities are simply the result of evolution, how can they be reliable measures of objective moral truth? Why

[10] http://www.quodlibet.net/articles/johnson-morality.shtml. [Accessed: 23 February 2014.

[11] Bloom, Paul, 2013. *Just Babies, The Origins of Good and Evil*. NY: Broadway Books.

[12] http://www.thenation.com/article/170334/do-you-only-have-brain-thomas-nagel [Accessed: 23 January 2014].

should evolution prefer the perception of moral truth to whatever happens to be advantageous for reproduction?"

This subject of an objective moral code is still being hotly debated, as a search of the Internet will show. I believe the evidence presented here is that an absolute objective moral code does exist, based on the evidence of NEA that shows the moral code did not evolve, that it is present in all humans, and it was put there by a supernatural act at the introduction of the *Homo sapiens*. All the other views are subjective opinions without any evidence. However, acceptance of absolute moral values requires the acceptance of the supernatural, and that may be the most difficult part.

Many atheists argue that they do not need God to have high morals. That is true, even though they do not realize their morals actually originated with God.

There are many other philosophical views on morality, which I am not going to cover in the limited space here. This point is that morality, its source and meaning, has been debated for centuries without consensus. Will the views presented here have any impact on the debate?

Conscience – Conscience is that inner feeling that one's conduct is right or wrong, based on their view of the moral code with a sense to do what is right. Essentially, everyone has a conscience; however, it will vary widely in degree. Conscience also did not evolve but was obtained by the principle of NEA.

Concept of a god - Essentially every society has in their belief system a concept of a supreme transcendent being or god. There are many different interpretations of the god of their beliefs. Some of the belief systems tend to be regional; however, many are global and form the major religions we have today. Some believe in many gods, while others believe in a monotheistic god. Many countries such as Russia and China, have at one time, tried to eliminate God from their societies, but they have only been partially successful.

The concept of God is further supported by research done with small children by various investigators. Dr. Olivera Petrovich, of Oxford University, has performed several studies on British and Japanese children and has concluded that infants are hard-wired to believe in a god, and that atheism has to be learned. One of the most interesting results was when Japanese children were asked where the first dog came from.[13] Their answer was, "Kamisama! (God) made it." The profound fact is that God, the creator, is not part of Japanese culture or philosophy, and God is not taught, but the child inherently believed God was the creator of dogs.[14] In addition, the children were asked where God was. Their answer was God was like air or a vapor. Is this not a child's interpretation of spirit?

Free Will – As discussed earlier, everyone has free will. I include it here again because of the close tie with

---

[13] Zwartz, Barney, 2008,. *Infants 'Have a natural belief in God'*. Available at: http:/www.smh.com.au/action/printArticle?id=167303. [Accessed: 20 January 2015].

[14] Bryant, Rebecca. An interview posted by Jason Goroncy. 2008. In the Beginning: An Interview with Olivera Petrovich, Available at http:/paternallife.wordpress.com/2008/07/28/in-the-beginning-an-interview-with-olivera-petrovich. [Accessed: 20 March 2014].

consciousness, conscience and the moral code. Free will is more like a privilege, rather than being an attribute.

All of these attributes are related and that keeps the normal person on track for good most of the time. The evil in the world comes about from those missing any of these attributes or having a warped view of them.

The Complete Human

The initial primary goal of this book, and the related research, was to better understand our consciousness and how it came about. That was accomplished, but what is more important is the realization of a more complete definition of humans and the story of how it came about. The results presented here not only include consciousness, but also include our moral code, our conscience, a concept of a god, and our free will, in addition to other unique attributes.

As you examine the five attributes; consciousness, the moral code, our conscience, free will and the sense of a god, you realize they are related and unique, and belong to a set I call the **Human Defining Set (HDS)**. They, in effect, define the modern human and show the clear distinction between the earlier instinctive-driven creatures. I call a human with the HDS the **Complete Human,** the ultimate being, created by God. Look at how these five attributes of HDS are related and work together.

Our consciousness with its creative imagination can think up all kinds of activities to do. Our free will allows us to choose which activity. The moral code gives us guidance on which activity is proper, and our conscience is the judge of bad choices that are made. God is the final judge of our activities. As the *Homo sapiens* transitioned from being an instinctive-driven creature, HDS took over the primary control of human activity. God created the Complete Human with the capability to be self correcting as they transitioned to a thinking creature with full consciousness. The question is, will they make the right decisions? The Complete Human is unique among all living creatures. Nothing else comes close.

The HDS meets the criteria of NEA; therefore, these attributes must have been the same in our ancient ancestors prior to the initial branching as the attributes existing today. That says each of these attributes were present in the first of the *Homo sapiens*. It is profound that we can know this, with a high certainty, about the ancient *Homo sapiens*. These complex attributes just appeared in the new *Homo sapiens* without any natural explanation. There was no Darwinian mechanism for these attributes to have evolved; these attributes provided no advantage to the early, simple creatures. Obviously, this was a supernatural event.

Since consciousness was suppressed by some means, and since all the other attributes, moral code, concept of God, conscience and free will, require consciousness, they in effect were also suppressed.

By now, you are probably thinking that there are many other attributes unique to humans, and you would be correct. In fact, there are too many to list. Using your own imagination, you can think of many of those attributes. And, you can also determine if they meet the NEA criteria and belong to the HDS. If the attribute you are considering is universal to all people around the world, then, it is fair to say it meets the NEA criteria and was supernaturally given to humans at their introduction, 200 kya.

There is one important attribute of humans I purposely left out of the attributes of consciousness, and that is emotion. I did so because I see emotion in some animals without consciousness, and therefore, felt it might not be unique to humans. My daughter once had a dog that was highly emotional. When she would leave the house, this dog must have felt their relationship was over, and she would never return. Then, when she did return, the dog would go berserk with happiness that she returned after all.

My feeling now is the emotion exhibited by animals is very basic, and probably was present in early humans. However, I believe that modern humans have a much higher level of emotion with many dimensions due to our consciousness. I further believe the higher level of emotion belongs in the set of HDS. Let me discuss several of these emotional attributes. One of the most important is the ability to love. The Greeks described love best with four different definitions: *Storge* is fondness as between family members, *Philia* is brotherly love between close friends, *Eros* is romantic love and *Agape* is "God-love" or unconditional love, which exists regardless of the circumstances. Given the universality of love in all societies, it is easy to see that it fits the criteria of NEA and was given to humans by God in the beginning. If humans have the ability to love, then they also must have the ability to hate. Why would God provide this?

The answer is simple. God could have easily programmed humans to just love Him, but He wanted more than just a robot. He wanted a thinking reasoning creature that was free to choose to either love Him or not.

Another attribute I want to introduce here is the concept of relationships. Humans in all societies migrate to having relationships with others. It is the rare individual that does not have some relationship. Like love, relationships have many different versions. We have a relationship with our spouse, family, friends, associates, and organizational members. We even have a one-sided relationship as fans of a sports team, a music group, or a famous person we admire. Both love and relationships, as described here, are unique to humans. Animals do not demonstrate the level as do humans.

It is said the human mind has a minimum of three basic functions: cognition, feelings, and volition.[15] The cognitive component is our consciousness, the thinking, analyzing, reasoning and figuring things out. The volition component is the driving force that sets our agendas, purposes, desires, motivations and will. We see free will exercised here.

Feeling is the emotion component that tells us how we are doing in a given situation. Emotions come from the

[15] Elder, Linda. 1996. *Critical Thinking and Emotional Intelligence*. Available at: https://www.criticalthinking.org/pages/cognition-and-affect-critical-thinking-and-emotional-intelligence/485. [Accessed: 30 April 2015].

subconscious mind,[16] and are hardwired in the brain.[17] Emotions are one of the most important attributes of humans. The emotional feelings range from happiness to sadness, from joy to sorrow, from satisfaction to frustration, from love to hate, and so on.[18] And, I believe that relationships are derived from emotions; feelings are what make relationships. It is the natural interaction with other humans, either in conversation, humor, debates, romance, competitions, either in group or one-on-one that make humans so interesting. It is perhaps the loving relationships that are the most significant, either with each other or with God. It is what God specifically asked of us – to love Him and our enemies as well.

In summary, what I have learned is that a supernatural event occurred when God created *Homo sapiens*, apparently as a new creature about 200kya. He gave this new being the HDS with all the many unique attributes and then, suppressed these attributes until the earth was totally populated. That is the Complete Human.

Adam and Eve Story

Since the discovery that *Homo sapiens* appeared about 200kya, there has been the discrepancy between this and the

---

[16] Radwan, M. F. *Where Do Emotions Come From?* Available at: http://www.2knowmyself.com/understanding_emotions/where_do_em otions_come_from. [Accessed: 30 April 2015].

[17] Koch, S. N. *Emotions are Hard-wired in the Brain.* MyBrainNotes.com. Available at: http://mybrainnotes.com/fear-rage-panic.html. [Accessed: 30 April 2015].

[18] Elder, op cit.

Biblical account of Adam and Eve. We do not know for sure when Adam and Eve lived, but a common time believed by many Biblical scholars is about 4,000 years BC.[19]

The significance of this time, 4,000 years BC, is essentially the same time I had earlier estimated for the end of the Sapient Breakout or the time humans acquired full consciousness and became the first Complete Humans. The first Complete Humans, Adam and Eve, were the first humans that had the consciousness suppression removed in about 4,000 BC, now making that Bible story consistent with the secular evidence. **Now, for the first time, the biblical time of the first humans, Adam and Eve, is the same as the secular estimate for the appearance of the first Complete Humans with full consciousness**. Now, I admit there is some conjecture in both the time of full consciousness and the biblical time of Adam and Eve, but it is significant in that if true, a major discrepancy between the Bible and secular history has now been resolved.

In addition, another problem with the Bible story was: **Who did the siblings of Adam and Eve marry? Now, we know that other humans (not yet with full consciousness) were around that they could marry and avoid incest**.

Also, there is strong evidence that the Garden of Eden was located at the northern end of the Persian Gulf. This is in agreement with the first event of full consciousness occurring in the Fertile Crescent. However, that area of the

---

[19]https://answers.yahoo.com/question/index?qid=20061001193714AAv 3qBH. [Accessed: 2 February 2015].

Garden is now under about 400 feet of water due to the rising water of the Ice Age melting. More details are presented in my first book.[20] Again, the Bible is now in agreement with secular history and evidence. The Book of Nature and the Book of Scripture are in agreement.

Many have thought that the Adam and Eve story in the Bible was just pure legend, but now, there is evidence that shows some parts of the story are a literal truth. My own belief in the story, as told to Moses in Genesis, was intended to be literal, but now, as we have gained more knowledge of human history and nature, the story as told still applies. Now, it is a combination of literal and symbolic truth. This takes a very clever author to create a story without contradiction, accurate at the time of Moses, and is still accurate for today with only adjustment of interpretation, just as only God could do. Also, this view now makes much more sense.

I say this Bible story is part symbolic because there were people living throughout the rest of the world at the time of Adam and Eve that had not yet realized their full consciousness. They could not have been direct blood descendents of Adam and Eve, since their ancestors migrated to their locations before Adam and Eve existed. However, they are symbolic descendants. I am one of those people. My ancient ancestors, according to the DNA tracking system, went through the Middle East long before

---

[20] Shaunfield, Wallace. 2010, *My God, Your God?* Boerne, Texas: Nealhas Publications.

Adam and Eve and were living in the European area at the time of this event.

This is not to say the Bible is wrong, but rather, we need to interpret what was being said correctly. I should point out that the early Bible stories were written for the people of the Middle East and biblical references to the whole Earth are referring to the world they knew at that time. It did not mean to include distant regions of the world such as the Americas. This is not based on my opinion, but rather, on other similar phrases in the Bible that use the same phraseology and are clear on the extent of what the whole Earth really meant. Hugh Ross provides several examples of scripture to show what the phrases such as "all the world" and "men of all nations" really meant in terms of location.[21] As one example, 1 Kings 4:34 says, "Men of all nations came to listen to Solomon's wisdom, sent by the kings of the world". 1 Kings 10:24 adds, "The whole world sought audience with Solomon to hear the wisdom God had put in his heart." The verses in 1 Kings 4:31 and 2 Chronicles 9 indicates the visitors came from as far away as Sheba, modern day Ethiopia and all the lands of Arabia. Apparently, the whole world in Solomon's day extended about 1,300 miles from Jerusalem. Ross provides several other examples to illustrate this point. This is important because the meaning of "whole Earth" and similar phrases throughout the Bible, such as the Noah flood, have been debated by Christians for centuries.

---

[21] Ross, Hugh. 2014. *Navigating Genesis*. Covina, CA: Reasons to Believe Press, pp. 146-147.

Human Soul

There is one other thought that may have occurred to you. The *Homo sapiens* without consciousness were much like the earlier ancestor species, an instinctive creature but with some higher level of capability. Consciousness and the other HDS (human defining set) attributes appeared to be a whole set of new attributes added to *Homo sapiens*, which greatly enhanced their capability.

Now, suppose this new capability is not part of the DNA or the brain directly, but added as a separate capability of the mind, such as the soul in the concept of duality. In fact, this concept of the HDS being independent of the brain is a strong argument for the concept of the soul. How was the HDS added to *Homo sapiens*? Did it become part of the DNA, or was it something entirely different? If HDS was in the DNA, think about how much change would be required to code all of the many attributes of HDS. While this concept of the HDS being the soul and not part of the brain, it still, in some way, uses the brain for the processing of thought, data, reason, etc. The early *Homo sapiens* without HDS were very similar to their ancestor species with the possible exception that their brain must have had more power to handle the added functionality of the HDS. This might be similar to the case where a new, powerful software program often requires a more powerful computer.

I have come to believe it is reasonable that the basic HDS is essentially our intellect and our soul. It is an entity that was not initially part of the *Homo sapiens* but was added. Could it not be easily separated to live on after death, just as in the afterlife as Christians believe? All of those mental abilities and the memories accumulated during life perfectly fit the description for the soul. In fact, this is the most reasonable explanation for the soul I have seen.

The Question of Evil

The Complete Human sounds like an ideal creature and if so, why is there evil in the world? It turns out that essentially everyone falls short on always meeting the full set of positive requirements of the Complete Human. Some come close, but others miss it by a very large degree. Adam and Eve were the first to violate the code set by God about not eating the forbidden fruit. They probably would not have done it if evil had not been present in the Garden. This illustrates how the distribution of good and bad for all people is shifted toward bad by evil forces that exist in the world.

We are all familiar with those figures in history that are totally missing one or more of the positive HDS attributes and are in effect incomplete humans. Hitler apparently had a limited moral code and no conscience. It is ironic that Hitler was trying to eliminate the imperfect humans when he was one of them. Stalin also apparently was missing the moral code and a conscience. Both Hitler and Stalin were deranged. However, these are not alone. The 20th century was the most bloody in all of human history. The book, *Atrocities,*[22] shows humans are the most deadly beings in history. All of these atrocities are the result of evil acts of people, and this evil occurred after humans transitioned from an instinctive creature to one with full consciousness. To give you an idea of the magnitude of these atrocities, I list a small sample of the associated deaths in recent wars:

- Second World War, 66,000,000
- First World War, 15,0000,000
- Vietnam War, 4,200,000
- Korean War, 3,000,000
- American Civil War, 695,000

Religion is not exempt from these atrocities. The most commonly cited and compared religious conflicts are the Crusades and Islamic activities.

The Crusades were a series of about nine military campaigns, supposedly to reclaim the Holy Land from the Muslim invaders.[23] They originated principally in Christian churches in Europe and took place in the years 1095 to 1272 AD. Many will defend the Crusades as just wars to reclaim the Holy Land from the Muslims. There may be some truth in that, but there were still atrocities committed against both Muslims and Jews, and I should note that these acts are contrary to the teaching of Jesus. The estimated number of

---

[22] White, Matthew. 2012 *Atrocities, The 100 Deadliest Episodes in Human History.* NY: W. W. Norton and Company.

[23] http://www.sharefaith.com/guide/christian-apologetics/myth-busters-in-apologetics.html. [Accessed 3/29/2015].

deaths associated with the Crusades ranges from one million to three million.[24,25]

Islam is responsible for a very large number of deaths due to their attempt to convert all people in the world to Islam. In addition, there have many deaths due to infighting within Islam between the Shia and Sunni sects. It is said that Muslims have killed more Muslims than anyone else. Since Islam was founded 1,400 years ago, the total number of deaths due to Islam possibly exceeds 250 million.[26] That number is about one hundred times that of the Crusades, so be aware of this when you see a comparison. That number is also about three times all the people killed in the recent major wars listed earlier. One reason the deaths caused by Islam is so high is the Quran, in numerous verses, teaches you should kill anyone who does not convert to Islam. In fairness to Islam, there are Muslims that say these verses are taken out of context, and these verses apply to special cases in Islamic history where Muslims were defending themselves.[27] However, the number of killings does seem excessive for just defense. Then, you

---

[24] *Ibid.*

[25] http://en.wikipedia.org/wiki/List_of_wars_and_anthropogenic_disasters_by_death_toll. [Accessed: 20 May 2015].

[26] http://www.americanthinker.com/articles/2014/05/the_greatest_murder_machine_in_history.html. [Accessed: 10 March 2015].

[27] http://www.alislam.org/egazette/updates/why-does-the-quran-say-that-infidels-should-be-killed/. [Accessed: 31 march 2015].

must ask if the Muslim's defense of Islam is in effect the lies that are permitted in the Quran to promote Islam.[28]

Abortion is another one of the evils in the human race. It is allowed in many civilized nations. The U.S. Supreme Court legalized abortion in 1973. "Super smart lawyers promoted with black robes" made this moral decision based on the right of pure convenience of the mother and total disregard of the right to life of the baby. Oliver Wendell Holmes Jr. (1809-1894), the famous and influential Supreme Court Justice, declared that morality and law have nothing to do with each other, and that every trace or hint of morality must be stripped from law.[29] His strong influence on the Supreme Court explains some of the decisions we have seen from the courts. So, should we look to lawyers, judges and the courts for moral guidance? From 1973 through May 2015, nearly 58 million legal abortions occurred.[30]

If you look at all the deaths in the last century due to evil, you may wonder if any of these people now missing from our society, might have found the cure for cancer and other diseases, eased human suffering, improved our education, contributed to world peace, or otherwise made

---

[28] http://www.muslimfact.com/bm/terror-in-the-name-of-islam/islam-permits-lying-to-deceive-unbelievers-and-bri.shtml. [Accessed: 14 April 2015].

[29] Whitney, David. *The Darwinization Of Law in America.* U.S. Constitution Course: Student Notes. Available at: http://www.theamericanview.com/wp-content/uploads/2013/05/The-Darwinization-Of-Law-In-America.pdf. [Accessed: 5 February 2015].

[30] http://www.numberofabortions.com/. [Accessed: 23 May 2015].

significant contributions to our society. The point of all this is that evil is present wherever humans exist, and we must always be on guard against it.

So, what is the answer to the question of evil? If we could assign a value for evil, and then plot the distribution of all people, I believe we would find a normal, bell-shaped curve with most people who are generally good in the center, and then on the edges, a few who were very good and a few who were inherently evil. However, because of strong supernatural evil forces present in the world, the curve would be shifted toward the evil direction. The best we can do is to try and do our best to be good, but we know we will not be totally successful. I have a theory that God is testing us humans with the presence of evil.

A Review of the Strength of the Evidence

As we come to the end of the story of how humans arrived at this point in time, there are two additional thoughts to consider. First, I would like to review the strength of the key evidence in the how of the story. The story is complex and is dependent on the truth of these key evidences. Then, in the next and final chapter, I would like to review what this story has yielded, the marvelous human.

The key evidences of the story of how humans developed are listed below:

- Based on architectural evidence, *Homo sapiens* appeared in Africa about 200kya.
- The most important piece of evidence shows the basic HDS set of attributes, consciousness, the

moral code, conscience, a sense of a god, and free will, plus many other attributes existed at the introduction of *Homo sapiens*. They just appeared without any natural explanation. This is very solid as it is based on the principle of NEA and points to a supernatural event.

- Next is the evidence that shows consciousness was suppressed as a supernatural event in the beginning. While it is clear that consciousness was suppressed, this means all the other attributes in HDS were also suppressed as part of the original supernatural event.

- There is evidence to support the idea that *Homo sapiens* were an entirely new creature, not evolved from previous *Homo* species. While this makes sense, the evidence is not strong.

- Around 70kya, there began a migration out of Africa, first into the Middle East, then Australia, and eventually all the continents of the whole Earth were inhabited by *Homo sapiens*. This is the first time any of the *Homo* species migrated to the Americas. This is supported by the DNA migration model and is strong evidence.

- There is strong evidence from the beginning throughout the history of humans that shows the early humans did have some limited levels of consciousness, which was possessed by the innovators of their day. This shows up in the various activities in early cave dwellers, the cave art of Europe, activities at Göbekli Tepe, and then, the early agriculture activities in the Fertile Crescent. Note that none of these early signs of consciousness resulted in full consciousness.

- Around 10kya, the Ice Age was coming to an end, the climate was moderating, and wild crops were flourishing. This allowed the hunter-gathers to settle down. This resulted in a rapid increase in population since the number of children was not limited by the number they could carry in their travels.

- Of all the early signs of consciousness, only that associated with agriculture survived and continued, while the other examples apparently died out. The reason agriculture survived in the Fertile Crescent and all around the world is that it provided the basic need of food, and as a result, a way for populations to increase, and then, move into other ventures. The evidence here is the unquestioned expansion of agriculture and population in the early Neolithic period that formed the foundation of susequent developments in society throughout the world.

- The switch to agriculture first occurred in the Fertile Crescent, and within 3,000 years, the population changed from a hunter-gatherer society to one fully dependent on agriculture.

- While the evidence clearly shows consciousness was initially suppressed, it is not totally clear as to how it later became expressed. However, we know it did become expressed over a period of time, first with the refinement of agriculture, and then, as activities expanded into other areas from agriculture. It is as if full consciousness was not needed until the range of interest and activities were broader than just the single focus of agriculture. And, then, it appears that consciousness emerged as it was needed.

- With full consciousness realized, we see the results of HDS come into play. We see the impact of the full range of free will being exercised, ranging from the great and good things to the horrific evils brought about by humans.

- The estimated time full consciousness was realized and humans became complete is about 4,000 BC, or about the same time as the Adam and Eve story. For the first time, we have agreement in the secular story of the first complete humans and the biblical story of the same event, assuming we treat the biblical story as part literal and part symbolic.

- With full consciousness realized in societies around the world, we see a rapid rise in population and development in advances such as buildings, writing, language, mathematics, literature, music, travel, art, communications, philosophy and all the attributes associated with an advanced civilization.

The story of how humans developed is fascinating and involved, not what you might first expect from either a secular or a spiritual perspective. The basic theme of the story of human development is based on solid evidence, and time will tell if it is accepted as true or not.

14 HUMANS, GOD'S CHILDREN

Now that we have a good idea of how humans arrived at the present state, let us look at what this story has wrought. Who are these creatures, *Homo sapiens,* also known as humans? Are we special or just the same kind but with a higher degree compared to other primates, as Darwin believed? Stephen Gould once remarked: "For if we could establish an unambiguous distinction-of kind rather than degree-between ourselves and our closest relatives, we might gain justification long sought for our cosmic arrogance."[1] That is the key question that humans have asked for centuries. The reason it is important is that if the answer is we are just a degree higher than primates, then Darwinian Evolution is likely true; however, if we are different in kind as well, then there is more than just evolution, and the supernatural and God must exist.

We now have evidence that the human brain has a feature not present in any other primate, and that makes humans different in kind. As stated earlier, in 2014, it was reported that a region of the brain was discovered called the lateral frontal pole prefrontal cortex, and it is believed to be unique to humans and may support distinctive cognitive

---

[1] Berlinski, David. 2009. *The Devil's Delusion*. NY: Basic Books. p.160.

abilities.[2,3] This new evidence strongly supports the view that *Homo sapiens* actually are a unique and special creature that are not only different in degree but also in kind.

And, there is even stronger evidence. Compared to other living creatures, humans are not the largest; they are not the strongest nor are they the fastest. However, humans are more superior because of their brain; it is more advanced in basic function, plus it has the added attributes of HDS. No other creature has consciousness, a moral code, a sense of a god, free will, plus many other unique attributes. This added set of attributes, the HDS, is believed by many to be the soul. The added property of HDS is enough to make the human different in kind. It is much more than just a greater degree.

The instinctive-driven creatures do quite well in their own environment; that is, until there is something out of the ordinary. Humans are masters of handling things out of the ordinary, and often, are the ones who created the unordinary things.

Humans are unique when it comes to our acquired language, our moral system, art, architecture, music, dance, mathematics, science, literature, government, travel, communication and religion to name a few, all the result of our consciousness. There seems to be no end to new

[2] Neubert eta al.Comparison of Human Ventral Frontal Cortex Areas for Cognitive Control and Language with areas in Monkey Frontal cortex. *Neutron* (2014), http://dx.doi,org/10.1016/j.neutron.2013.11.012.
[3] http://www.livescience.com/42897-unique-human-brain-region-found.html.

concepts and thoughts that occur daily. I cannot even begin to describe the extent of human activity, even if I devoted all of the 42,000 words of this book to the subject. You will have to use your own imagination to get a feel for the magnitude of the subject. We do observe a universal sense of joy occurring when a new development is announced. Does anyone believe these achievements could be the result of unguided, random processes? If you do, you need to look again at what unguided random means.

One question that remains is: Do all people on Earth, including those in the few isolated primitive tribes, have full consciousness? There is the classic story of where an infant from a primitive tribe is adopted, raised in an advanced society and educated in a fine university with the result being that there is no difference between that child and the one born into the advanced society. Alfred Wallace, co-creator of the theory of naturalistic evolution, argues that characteristic human abilities must be latent in primitive man, existing somehow as an unopened gift.[4] This concept is similar to the thought I discussed where consciousness was present in early humans, but not yet expressed. I believe Wallace's thought of an **unopened gift** also adequately describes the mind as it relates to the potential of human achievement.

Humans are also noted for being busy; there seems to be something different going on all the time with humans. Part of this is due to an imagination to think up things to do,

---

[4] Ibid., p.159.

and then, the free will to select which ones. The list of activities humans engage in seems endless. It is said that the English language has between 25,000 and 100,000 verbs.[5] I suspect humans are probably involved with most of them in addition to activities that involve combinations of verbs. The activities can be either good or evil actions, and humans are not always good at making the proper choices.

Now consider this: Given all the activities that humans are engaged in, would it be possible to pre-program an instinctive brain with all the possible situations that might be encountered? I believe the answer should be clear – there is no way that the human brain has the memory capability for such a feat. However, just as God designed us, we do have the capability to analyze each situation and make decisions about our actions. The actions may not always be the best one, but at least, there is a process to do the right thing.

While all innovations have not been an improvement for society, essentially all problems with new innovations are the result of misuse by evil people. Wars are a result of evil people using advances in technology to try to bring about their worldview, and that has resulted in increased massive killings as technology has increased.

If you were to form your view of the state of evil based on the evening news, you would conclude that evil is all there is. However, I do not think that is the case, and as indicated earlier, I believe most people are generally good;

---

[5] http://www.wordwizard.com/phpbb3/viewtopic.php?f=16&t=8473. [Accessed: 11 May 2015].

although, all humans do sin. While human actions are shifted toward evil, there is still a great deal of good that goes on throughout the country and world each day and is not widely reported. That good shows up in special acts of love and caring that people have for each other. Churches and other service organizations have extensive outreach programs that provide shelter, clothing, food, tutoring and medical needs to countless people in need around the world. The amount of volunteer work to support these activities is impressive.

In addition to these special activities, you have the majority of people who go to work each day and perform their job doing some useful activity, which benefits society in some manner. This includes such a broad range of activities, too large to list them all, but includes truck drivers, clerks, medical research personnel, engineers, scientists, artists, teachers, repairmen, construction workers, police and firemen, doctors, nurses, pilots, architects, designers, child care workers, reporters, writers, and many other people behind the scenes, and the list goes on and on. All of these people are doing a job that is beneficial and good for our society. We all benefit in some way from their efforts. The fact that all of this work is done in harmony by millions of people speaks to the good in them.

However, there is much more about humans than just their actions of being good or bad. The one outstanding feature that makes humans unique is their imagination and creativity. All advancements in our civilization were the result of the creativity of the innovators throughout the ages. Keep in mind that anyone who comes up with a new idea, thought or concept is an innovator. It is the result of imaginations that make humans fascinating.

It is these innovations that allowed the population to increase beyond anything before. The population of the ancestor *Homo* species was maybe in the millions, while the population of *Homo sapiens* is now around seven billion. This fits the concept of first testing a design with prototypes, and when the design is finalized, you go into volume production.

We have shown humans are unique creatures unlike any other living thing. We are orders of magnitude more complex in degree, as well as being different in kind. However, the fact that many of the parts are similar to those in other primates suggests a common designer was involved.

If the solid logic presented here and the resulting story is true, then, this is a strong objective argument for the existence of God. Think about that.

Summary

The fascinating story of how early *Homo sapiens* became the modern humans we are today has now been told. Key discoveries were made that have a profound significance in understanding the history of humans. This study has been an examination of ourselves, which is always hard to do, and some might say, it is impossible to do in an objective manner. Previously, we have looked at the attributes we all have in common, and have wondered where they came from. Such things as the source of the moral code have been debated for centuries. We have also looked at the first *Homo sapiens* and wondered who they really were and how they became us.

The breakthrough that allowed this story to be told came about with the realization of the principle of the Non-Evolving Attribute (NEA). This allowed us to know the attributes of the first *Homo sapiens* with an uncanny degree of accuracy and confidence. There is no other analysis technique that comes close in producing these results. The early attributes I defined as the Human Defining Set (HDS) includes consciousness, the moral code, our conscience, the sense of a god, the ability to love and hate, plus a long list of other attributes we humans have in common today. The profound fact is that we know these many complex attributes were present in the early *Homo sapiens*. The question now is: How do we interpret this fact? How did these attributes get there? How does a naturalist interpret this fact? That could be difficult.

However, being a Christian theist, the explanation is quite easy. It should be clear that by following the evidence, wherever it leads, results in the fact that the appearance of the HDS in the first *Homo sapiens* was a supernatural event. And since it was a supernatural fact, it tells us that God was involved, and the event actually was God placing humans on Earth. We also know what attributes God gave the early humans, which are the same attributes we still have today. **I believe the event of the appearance of the first *Homo sapiens* is one of the most important events in all of human history, and I have explained how it happened.**

Throughout the centuries, men have filled volumes with conjecture about these things we now know with a great deal of certainty. Has God revealed something about Himself that we did not know before? It was as if God made a list of things He wanted in this new creature, humans. Among other things, He wanted a creature He could love, and one that would love Him back. He could have easily made us to love Him unconditionally, but that would not have been genuine love. For humans to truly love God, they must have the freedom to not love Him. God took a risk, knowing that some would reject His love. But, there was no other choice if God truly loved us.

This insight we get by NEA provides a unique look at the attributes God created in us. And, it is with the same detail and understanding we have by examining those same attributes that we have today. This is brand new knowledge we have about God that we did not have before.

One example of this is the evidence that suggests HDS appears to be our soul. The HDS has all the attributes you would expect to find in our soul. Could this really be true?

In addition, there is some evidence the *Homo sapiens* were new creatures without any ancestors from which they evolved. It does make some sense to add the HDS, apparently our soul, to a new creature rather than one that had just evolved from previous *Homo* species.

I believe humans today with HDS define the Complete Human.

All of this shows that humans are unique creatures both in degree and in kind. We also know humans are unique because as John Lennox, Oxford mathematics professor and prominent Christian, has said: "*God became one*".

It should be clear that you, a human who is reading this book, are one of those marvelous creatures that God created to be one of **God's Children**, and that is good. This is illustrated in the Bible, in Genesis 1: God created the universe and the world, and said it was good. It became <u>very good</u> when God placed man on Earth. What more is there to say?

Have a blessed day,
Shaun

EPILOGUE

This book is now complete with my thoughts now in sentences on paper. The research and writing of this book has been an activity of discovery and revelation. The original goal was to complete the story I began in my earlier books of how early *Homo sapiens* became the modern humans we are today. I long had the somewhat revolutionary view that the difference was that modern humans had the attribute of consciousness, while the early humans were instinctive-driven creatures. If that is true, then, when did we acquire consciousness? The approach to determine the answer was to use the scientific method of using secular data and logic and following the evidence, wherever it leads. I did meet the goal, and developed an understanding of how humans became the modern people we are today.

However, as often happens in research, much more was discovered – two specific things: 1) I discovered the set of attributes, HDS (Human Defining Set) that define the Complete Human, and which make humans different from all other life forms, and 2) The end results ended with an unexpected supernatural event, implying an Intelligent Designer or God was involved. While it is not possible to analyze a supernatural event, we can at least recognize one when it occurs; the laws of nature cannot explain the result.

Often in research, new tools have to be developed, and that happened here. Key to the success of this study was the realization of a novel logic principal, NEA (Non-Evolving Attributes). Simply stated, the principal says that if you have a group of isolated descendants from a common ancestor that have a common attribute that is the same for all descendants, then, that attribute could not have randomly evolved, because if it evolved in any one branch, it would have had to evolve the same in all branches, and that is impossible. Therefore, that attribute was present in the original ancestor. This simple principle allowed me to look at attributes common to isolated groups around the world and, with a high level of certainty, determine the attributes of their original ancestors.

What are the key additional attributes that make humans different and that were acquired at the appearance of humans on Earth about 200kya? (Note that while these attributes were present in the early *Homo sapiens*, we now know they were initially suppressed).

- Consciousness and the many attributes of consciousness explain many of the differences as I suspected, and it is the strongest attribute.
- The moral code, where we inherently know right from wrong.
- A free will to choose our actions.
- A conscience which provides self-guidance about our decisions and actions.

- The universal sense there is a god or some supreme being.
- The ability to love and also hate.
- The ability to have strong relationships and form societies.

It is interesting to note that these facts are well known to Christians from the Bible; however, it is profound that this is the first time these attributes have been realized using secular evidence and analysis. We now have agreement between the Book of Nature and the Book of Scripture on these important topics.

To give you an idea of how important this is, consider, as an example, the source of the moral code. Essentially, all people agree we have an inherent sense of what is right and wrong. The debate throughout the centuries has been about the source of the moral code. Atheists and naturalists argue that the moral code evolved or that it was created by individual or cultures, because of the benefit to society. However, it is clear from NEA that it could not have evolved, nor was it created by humans; but, instead, it came from God, as He wrote in on the hearts of all humans.

I should point out that the essential elements of this story are based on rock-solid logic with essentially no conjecture. You end up at a point where you have a supernatural event; there is no natural explanation for the situation. It is at that point, that I conclude the most reasonable answer is that an Intelligent Designer, or God, is responsible. These points in the story are when life originated on Earth and when humans were introduced on Earth. In both events, a believer would expect God to have been involved. You may have a different explanation, but I ask, does your story fit the evidence?

As an intriguing thought, what I find interesting is that originally Darwinism/naturalism was the advocate of science to verify their position, while theism was falsely believed to be unscientific, superstitious, and relegated to blind faith. In reality, what we find is that science is being used to confirm the theistic and Intelligent Design world view, while naturalism is on the defensive and is reduced to making subjective and dogmatic claims without any sound objective basis.

It is interesting that as this book was in final review, a new TV series, *FIRST PEOPLE*, began on PBS. It covers the history of humans at a more detailed level but does not give specifics as to how we first appeared other than to suggest it was evolution and interbreeding with ancient humans. The program does not consider consciousness as a factor. However, it is interesting, and I recommend it if there is a rerun.

One last thought: if the two supernatural events, the origin-of-life and the introduction of humans on Earth, were truly an act of God, then these two events are new apologetic[1] evidences for the existence of God!

---

[1] Christian apologetics – the discipline of defending the Christian faith with evidence, reason, philosophical arguments and other information.

Appendix A: Supernatural, Evolution, Truth

The text of this book touches on several areas of controversy; the supernatural, evolution, naturalism, and truth. These topics need further discussion because of their use in the text and also, because they typically are at ground-zero of controversy. I think it is appropriate that the reader understand my position on these important topics.

If you have read this far, you probably know, I was a devout atheist for many years. I formed the opinion at age 18 that there was no God, based on my own analysis without any reading or input from anyone. I held that view of an 18-year old for many years. Then, after a careful objective study, I realized there was an abundance of secular evidence to support the fact that God does exist. In fact, my last book focuses on some of that evidence.[1] However, because of my long period of non-belief, I do have an understanding of that position and have the utmost respect for the atheist viewpoint.

Also, be aware, I am a retired electrical engineer, and my career was in research and development. My work involved and depended on applied science. I am a strong believer in going where the evidence leads, as is the only thing that works when you are carrying a scientific

---

[1] (Shaun). 2012. *GOD Exists! Ten Evidences for Belief.* Boerne, TX: Nealhas Publications.

hypothesis to a reliable and useful device, as I did in my career. Now retired, I still have a strong interest in scientific advances and have time for a broader area of interest. Earlier, as an atheist, I had the view that science and God were in conflict and took the view that science always won in any conflict. Now, I realize that belief was wrong, and I can find no area where science and God are in conflict.

Supernatural

A supernatural event is one that departs from what is usual or normal, especially so as to appear to transcend the laws of nature. This, I believe, is the most appropriate definition for this discussion.[2] The result of such an event is that our laws of science do not apply. We cannot understand such an event using scientific methods. While we do not have the ability to scientifically analyze beyond the event, we can at least recognize that a supernatural event has occurred. Recognition is fairly easy. It is obvious when certain things appear without an obvious cause. Should not our goal of any investigation be the truth? We should use the scientific method up to the point that it encounters the supernatural and then, switch our method of analysis to philosophy or whatever gives us the truthful answer. The origin-of-life in Appendix B is a classic example of such an analysis where the supernatural is encountered. The complex DNA coding system just appeared in the first life on Earth. To one who believes in a theistic God, this is totally expected; God

---

[2] http://www.merriam-webster.com/dictionary/supernatural. [Accessed: 18 April 2015]

introduced life on Earth, just as you would expect. And, there is a similar example in the appearance of humans with the attribute set of consciousness, the moral code, conscience and a sense of a god. Again, this is an expected supernatural action of a theistic God.

The people who have a problem with anything supernatural are typically naturalists. Some of the many different versions of naturalism are presented here.[3] The philosophy of **Metaphysical Naturalism** is the belief that nature is all that exists and that supernatural events do not exist. **Methodological Naturalism** is the belief that observable events in nature are explained by natural causes, without assuming either the existence or non-existence of the supernatural. **Absolute Methodological Naturalism** is the view that it is impossible for any empirical method to discover supernatural facts, even if there are some. **Contingent Methodological Naturalism** is the view that empirical methods are far more likely to uncover natural facts than supernatural ones, but it would not be impossible to confirm them empirically if any were found. This seems to be the most objective definition; although, it is probably the least popular. There are many other definitions of naturalism that I will not discuss. It is interesting that naturalists spend so much energy on the supernatural, which they do not believe exists. They have absolutely no evidence that the supernatural does not exist; therefore, such a view of the supernatural is just a subjective opinion.

---

[3] http://www.philosophybasics.com/branch_naturalism.html. [Accessed: 7 March 2015].

As I indicated above, detecting a supernatural event is easy. If there were no supernatural events, then, the naturalist would appear to be correct. However, how would a naturalist react to the solid, logical cases in the origin-of-life and appearance of human examples? Would they ignore the results or admit they did not understand? Or, would they admit that this must be an example of the supernatural? Such an event would present a major problem in the worldview of a naturalist. I suspect many naturalists have such a strong opinion that there are no supernatural events, and that opinion overrides the concept of following the evidence wherever it leads. They let an opinion come before the evidence. That being the case, they are poor scientists, and I wonder what other opinions are allowed to influence their results.

I find it interesting that naturalists depend so heavily on nature and wonder where they think the laws of nature and the order of nature comes from. Do they believe they are the result of some random unguided process? For those with an atheist view, I also wonder if seeing the truth in these examples, should not make you think maybe a reassessment of your position with an objective perspective is in order.

Darwinian Evolution

Darwinian Evolution is another topic that has been long debated and is one which is encountered in the story of humans. My opinion of evolution has vacillated since I wrote my first book in 2009. At that time, I began a serious look at the theory of Darwinian Evolution, and my first response was that evolution was the method God must have used to create all the many creatures on Earth – He would use some system to do it automatically and only intervene when He wanted something special. This was hardly a new thought, as it was the same as that of Asa Gray, a Harvard professor of botany and Charles Kingsley, vicar of Eversley, Hampshire. Both communicated with Darwin on the subject about the time Darwin's book, *On the Origin of Species*, was published in 1859.[4,5]

When Darwin's book was published, many adopted the view that life originated and propagated in nature and that God was not now necessary, and therefore, did not exist. Even if evolution were true, what about all the other things that God did, such as the creation of the universe, the origin-of-life and creation of nature itself? I believe that those who are atheist use Darwin's theory as a basis for their belief. If Darwin's evolution was shown to be false, they would have a problem with reduced support for their opinion about atheism. Darwin never claimed to be an atheist, but he acted like one. He had exposure to many people who accepted his theory, and yet they remained believers. Alfred Wallace, the coauthor of the theory of evolution, maintained his faith, while Darwin apparently did

---

[4] Charles Darwin and Asa Gray discuss Theology and Design. The American Scientific Affiliation.
http://www.asa3.org/ASA/PSCF/2001/PSCF/20001/PSCF901Miles.html, September 2001.
[5] Letter 2534 – Kingsley, Charles to Darwin. C. R. 18 Nov 1859, http://www.darwinproject.ac.uk/darwinletters/entry-2534.html.

not. It is interesting that both men had doubts: Darwin had doubts because of the consequences of the theory being true, while Wallace, considering the consequences, suspected his theory might be false.[6] It seems to me that Wallace was the more objective one of the two.

At the time Darwin published his theory, the DNA molecule had not been discovered. The changes we see today in evolution are believed to be due to mutations in the DNA, and the theory is now referred to as **Neo-Darwinism**.

By the time I wrote my second book in 2012, and after reading more on the subject, I began to have doubts about evolution in general. There were areas where Darwinian Evolution seemed to be the best explanation for the changes in life. However, there were other areas where Darwin's theory did not fit the evidence, and that a supernatural event was the most reasonable explanation.

Intelligent Design (ID)

A supernatural event appears to be the action of a transcendent, all powerful, intelligent designer. The people in the **Intelligent Design (ID)** community would stop here, and just suggest the event of DNA being present in the original life form on Earth was a supernatural or ID event and not go farther as to suggest a god was involved. Their argument is that the events up to a conclusion of ID are a

---

6 Berlinski, David. 2009. *The Devil's Delusion.* NY: Basic Books, p157.

scientific issue, and to suggest a god was involved is a philosophical issue.

I completely support the ID approach to the issues at hand and believe their answers to questions are the only reasonable ones. However, since I am interested in the complete story, I will cross over that line and suggest that the intelligent designer is God and that He initiated life on Earth and used DNA as the life- coding system. It is perfectly reasonable to expect that a theistic God would initiate life on Earth, and that is exactly what we see. This is the only viable solution I see to the fundamental questions in the origin-of-life: How was the complex DNA encoding system, as well as the complex information code in the DNA, created naturally without aid from an intelligent being?

In recent years, the Discovery Institute has been the main organization promoting the Intelligent Design movement, and they have presented a number of scientific, and logical critiques of some of the basic tenants of evolution. They have raised numerous concerns for Darwinian Evolution and presented many solid cases for intelligent design. Three classic examples are: *Darwin's Black Box* by Michael Behe,[7] *Darwin's Doubt,* Stephen Meyer,[8] and *Icons of Evolution* by Jonathan Wells.[9] There are many others.

---

[7] Behe, Michael, 1996. *Darwin's Black Box.* NY: Free Press.
[8] Meyer, Stephen, 2013. *Darwin's Doubt.* NY: Harper One.
[9] Wells, Jonathan, 2000. *Icons of Evolution.* Washington, DC: Regnery Publishing, Inc.

More information about the Discovery Institute is available at their website.[10]

Cambrian Explosion

One of the major areas of debate is the Cambrian Explosion, the well-known burst of diversification of life that started 543 mya and lasted five million years.[11] During this short period, nineteen of the forty known phyla (body plans) made their appearance during this period. It appears these new life forms just appeared without any obvious ancestors. This is after three billion years of little change in life since it originated on Earth. Even more significant than the number of phyla is the orders of magnitude of additional information in the DNA required to define the much more advanced life forms. The basic problem with the Cambrian Explosion is you have all these new life forms without any apparent ancestors.

Darwin was aware of the problem and stated the lack of ancestral forms was a valid argument against his theory. He anticipated that the missing evidence would be found. However, that has not happened, and instead, additional new advance life forms have been discovered since Darwin's time, making the issue even bigger.[12] Because of the significance of this to the naturalist's and the atheist's view,

---

[10] http://www.discovery.org/. [Accessed: 30 May 2015].

[11] Meyer, S. et. al. *The Cambrian Explosion: Biology's Big Bang*. Available at: http://www.discovery.org/scripts/viewDB/filesDB-download.php?id=29. [Accessed: 28 April 2015].

[12] http://www.darwinsdilemma.org/pdf/faq.pdf. [Accessed: 4/28/2015]

they have presented numerous theories, trying to explain this apparent dilemma. One argument the naturalists have made is that the ancestors were soft bodies and did not leave any fossils that survived. However, many soft-body fossils have survived in the very layers below the advanced life forms where you would expect to find the ancestors. A sample of two articles that defend the naturalist view is listed and more are found on the internet.[13,14] The members of the Discovery Institute argue the most reasonable explanation for the Cambrian Explosion is Intelligent Design.

It seems to me that the stronger side of this debate is Intelligent Design; however, I am happy with either viewpoint. If ID is correct, then the advent of the new animal types was a supernatural act of God, and if Darwin's evolution is true, then evolution was the system initiated God.

Other Darwinian Evolution Problems

While there is an abundance of evidence for microevolution (the small changes that occur within a species), there is a serious lack of evidence for macroevolution, the creation of new species of life, and that is after 150 years of searching.

---

[13] Does the Cambrian Explosion Pose a Challenge to Evolution? http://biologos.org/questions/cambrian-explosion. [Accessed: 28 April 2015].

[14] Sudden Appearance? http://ncse.com/creationism/analysis/sudden-appearance. [Accessed: 28 April 2015].

One problem with Darwin's theory of gradual change is that most all creatures we see today have been around typically for a hundred thousand years or more without any of the gradual change, described by Darwin. This is the principle of stasis, which exhibits little or no change over long periods of time. Creatures have an uncanny, digital-like, lack of change. For example, some shark families have been in existence for 150 million years without any change.

To address this problem, Stephen Gould and Niles Eldridge, in 1972, proposed the theory of **punctuated equilibrium**, which states (macro) evolution occurs in rapid spurts interspersed with long periods of stasis.[15] This would answer the problem of the lack of intermediate fossils; however, this theory has not been accepted by all evolutionists. And, there is a problem with this concept, because large, rapid, random changes in the DNA usually are rejected by the cell.

There are several key questions that need answered to determine the feasibility of such a theory. How many mutations are typically required for a species change? Is this number of mutations practical in a short period of time? What is the probability of an occurrence with this number of mutations?

Instead of addressing the questions and criticisms about Darwinian Evolution scientifically and professionally, the Darwinists do not like anyone questioning their opinions.

---

[15] http://www.conservapedia.com/Punctuated_equilibrium. [Accessed: 29 April 2015].

They have gone to great lengths to suppress any thoughts along this line, including: denying tenure, firing people, seeking court judgments that state ID is religion and cannot be taught in public schools. The movie, *Expelled - No Intelligence Allowed* with Ben Stein highlighted some of the tactics used by the Darwin evolutionists. The highly respected *Nature* magazine even recently admitted that scientists suppressed criticisms of neo-Darwinism to avoid lending support to Intelligent Design.[16]

I am not aware of any other field in science where there has been such tactics used. What is the reason for this? I believe emotions run high because the field involves science, religion, atheism, and the fact that Darwinian Evolution has been around for over 150 years, and there are still many unanswered questions. Furthermore, Darwinian Evolution is the basis for their atheistic views, and if it were to be proven wrong, then they would have a problem with their world view.

Many of the scientists in the field are staunch naturalists and atheists and have the opinion that the supernatural does not exist. A recent Pew Research survey showed 98% of AAAS (American association for the Advancement of Science) scientists believe humans and other living things evolved over time.[17] However, a similar survey by the National Center for Science Education,

---

[16] http://www.evolutionnews.org/2014/10/nature_admits_s090321.html. [Accessed: 20 January 2015].

[17] Pew Research Center, January 29,2015,"Public and Scientists Views on Science and Society".

completed in 1997, agreed with the Pew survey, but added that forty percent of biologists, mathematicians, physicians, and astronomers include God in the process.[18]

It seems to me we could eliminate or reduce the polarization that exists in the field of evolution if we would sit down and work together to answer many of the existing questions. There is so much to be discovered. I see some evidence this is happening in recent articles. Two examples include: *Does Evolutionary Theory Need a Rethink?*[19] and *Still Taking Aim at Eric Metaxas, the Media Underestimate the Degree to Which Physicists See Evidence for Intelligent Design.*[20]

This might be possible if we follow the classic scientific approach used in research. That approach is to follow the evidence wherever it leads, always seeking the truth. Then, I would add the thought that if the study crosses the line between science and religion, then, so be it. In fact, such an event adds to the understanding of both the science and God. Of course, an atheist would have a problem with this.

My view of evolution has stabilized based on the evidence presented in this book. First of all, it is clear from the evidence that God is involved with evolution; He initiated the simple, single cell life form on Earth using DNA as the system to control life and the reproduction of life.

---

[18] http://ncse.com/rncse/17/6/many-scientists-see-gods-hand-evolution. [Accessed: 18 April 2015].

[19] Laland, K. and Wray, G. 2014. Does Evolutionary Theory Need a Rethink? *Nature*. Vol. 514. Pp.161-164.

[20] http://www.evolutionnews.org/2015/01/still_taking_ai092671.html. [Accessed: 20 January 2015].

Given that, I think it's reasonable to assume God would stay involved, and He must have created the system of evolution that was common during the first three billion years of life on Earth. When we come to the Cambrian Explosion, I doubt that evolution could account for the many, new complex forms, and while I have no evidence, I suspect God intervened in creating much of the variety of life we see today. I also suspect that the evolution system God created continued to operate, and God only intervened when He wanted a major change that evolution could not provide. As stated earlier, I suspect the *Homo* species that preceded *Homo sapiens* were design prototypes that God used in designing *Homo sapiens*. Remember that there is evidence that *Homo sapiens* were a completely new creation and did not evolve.

In summary, my model of evolution involves both nature and the supernatural or God. While I cannot totally rule out Darwin's model of gradual evolution, I believe if it exists, it is only a minor part of evolution we observe today. That is what I clearly see in the evidence.

Appendix B: NEA, Origin-of-life

As I went through the research for my last book, I had the realization of a very profound fact: Populations today, although isolated by thousands of miles, have many identical complex attributes. How did this happen? Darwinian Evolution could not have been the reason, as you shall see soon. These attributes must have been there from the very beginning. In my last book, I was presenting the case that God exists and in Chapter 9, *Origin-of-life*, I used what I then called the **Non-evolving DNA Argument.**[1] I have now made the concept more general, and call it the principle **of Non-Evolving Attributes, (NEA)**.

Non-Evolving Attributes (NEA)
- If there is a population with many different groups separated by distance and/or time and all members have evolved through many different branches from a common ancestor,
- and if all members have a common identical attribute, then that attribute could not have randomly evolved, because if there was random evolution in any one branch that attribute would have had to

---

[1] Shaunfield, Wallace (Shaun). 2012. Origin-of-life. In: *GOD Exists! Ten Evidences for Belief.* Boerne, TX: Nealhas Publications. pp. 83-88.

evolve in the same exact manner in each branch and that is impossible.

- Therefore, if there was no evolution, then the original ancestor would have the same identical attribute.

Note that if the evolution is by a specific rule, then, the evolution is deterministic, and it is expected that the end attributes of the entities will be the same with the normal variation of process.

The principle of NEA is best understood with an example, and we will look at the origin-of-life question. It follows these logical steps:

- Fact: all present forms of life on Earth (except for some viruses that use RNA) use the same coding – the complex DNA coding system.

- Once branching started in the tree of life, there could have been no change or evolution in the DNA coding system that defines the species and reproduction instructions. If there had been a change in any one branch that same exact change would have had to happen in all branches, and that is essentially impossible.

- Therefore, if there was no evolution in the DNA coding system, then the original simple, life form would have used the same complex DNA coding system we have today.

- For the simple original life form to have had the complex DNA coding system must have been a supernatural event that required an intelligent designer, God.

Note that the actual code will change as the various species appear, but the DNA coding system could not change.

Origin-of-life

This whole logic scheme is so simple and obvious that I cannot believe it has not been presented earlier. Surely, if it had it would have attracted more attention. However, I am not aware this concept has been presented earlier.

In this origin-of-life example used to illustrate NEA, we have an event where the most reasonable explanation for the DNA coding, being present in the original primitive life forms, is that it is obviously a supernatural event, based on the definition of a supernatural event. The event has no natural explanation. The only viable explanation is intelligent design.

This is profound: **I believe the question of the origin-of-life has finally been answered with secular evidence. God introduced life on Earth, just as known by believers all along.** Furthermore, it is highly unlikely that humans will ever be able to reproduce this event with just natural forces. There are two reasons for this conclusion: 1) The DNA coding system is very complex, and there is no basis for it to just appear naturally and 2) for the system to work, information is required within the coding system, and that must come from an intelligent source. Intelligence does not just pop into existence from nature. This is the first secular evidence that confirms the facts about the origin-of-life, known all along by believers,.

The basic fact is scientists have no clue as to how life originated on Earth. This is evidenced by their actions. They have tried to create life by mixing the various chemicals of life, applying an electrical discharge, and various other processes. I see no consideration of the vast amount of information contained in each cell. Can you create information out of chemistry? Their actions remind me of the alchemist of earlier days and the fictional attempts of Dr. Frankenstein. As least, Dr. Frankenstein started with material that was once alive.

Tree of Life in Question

The above discussion was based on a simple tree of life with a single common ancestor as proposed by Darwin. This has been a good model for the discussion of NEA; however, evolutionists have never been able to construct a meaningful tree of life – the data just does not fit a tree format. Numerous papers in recent years have addressed this issue, and the consensus is that a more accurate model is a complex network instead of a simplistic tree. However, while a network is a more accurate model, it is not perfect.[2] The reason is that biology is much more complex than originally thought, due to things such as crossbreeding, and genetic swap among others.[3] Another factor that evolutionists do not often discuss is the Cambrian Explosion where new animals appeared without any apparent ancestors. They became the first of a long series of descendants. How does all this affect the NEA model?

First of all, there is consensus that there still was a single common ancestor (except for the Cambrian Explosion creatures). Therefore, I believe the NEA model is now even stronger than the simple tree model. There could have been no evolution of the DNA coding system, especially with a more complex network mode. Therefore, as concluded in the simple tree model, the initial life form appearing with the DNA coding system was a supernatural event brought about by the intelligent designer, God.

The Cambrian Explosion is an even stronger argument for an intelligent designer. It appears that the new animals that appeared during the Cambrian Explosion were the first of their species, without ancestors, and they appeared much later in the time that life has been present on Earth. Since these independent life forms all had

---

[2] Sample, Ian. Evolution: *Charles Darwin was wrong about the tree of life.* http://www.theguardian.com/science/2009/jan/21/charles-darwin-evolution-species-tree-life. [Accessed: 26 May 2015].

[3] *Demolishing Darwin's Tree: Eric Bapteste and the Network of Life.* http://www.evolutionnews.org/2013/09/demolishing_dar076431.html. [Accessed: 26 May 2015].

descendants that used the DNA coding, they also used the DNA coding system, and that required an intelligent designer, God, to select DNA as the coding system for each new creature.

Panspermia

With the sudden appearance of life, it may appear to some that this is evidence of panspermia. Panspermia is the theory that life has been seeded throughout the universe by propagation of seeds of life or bacteria, or their spores that move from planet to planet by asteroids or other bodies. It is not a new concept; Bernoit de Mallet in 1743 wrote about the theory of panspermia.[4] More recently, Nobel prizewinner, Francis Crick, suggested that life on Earth was the result of direct panspermia where bacteria are transported in protective shields by intelligent agents. Lithopanspermia is the more popular version, and that is where bacteria are transported within protective rocks being expelled into space by activities such as volcanic action on the planet.[5] This has some credibility, since there is evidence that bacteria can withstand the extreme environment of space.

However, there is a paradox in that theory. Celeb A. Scharf raises the question: If these life-bearing spores can exist in outer space, then we should expect to see them everywhere; on the Moon, Mars, Europa, and all the other

---

[4] http://www.panspermia-theory.com/.
[5] Ibid.

bodies in space.[6] And we do not see this. Furthermore, if life originated on Earth by this method, then we should expect to see life originating at numerous locations on Earth instead of a single location in Africa. What chance is there that spores only landed in one spot on Earth?

Furthermore, are we to believe that life, as defined by the complex and robust DNA coding and decoding system, may have evolved by some natural means on some other planet, and then when it arrived on Earth, it went through trillions of generations without any further evolution?

I see panspermia as an attempt to remove God from the equation of life. Does anyone think that by transferring the event to another planet that diminishes the involvement of God?

There is another strong argument that reduces the probability that life originated on Earth by transfer from another planet. If you look at the time involved for an alien planet to form and begin to have life, and then the time for life to be transferred to Earth, those planets have to be relatively close to Earth compared to the size of the universe. That significantly limits the number of planets that could be candidates for having life that is transferred to Earth. In addition, while the number of planets out there may be large, the number that could support life is rather small. And, when you look at the unique features of planet Earth, you

---

[6] http://blogs.scientificamerican.com/life-unbounded/2012/10/15/the-panspermia-paradox/. [Accessed: 21 September 2013].

realize that Earth might be a rare one-of-a kind body.[7] In that case, there would be no other planets that would have the life to be transferred.

Let us look at the concept of panspermia using logic applied to the following list of possible options for panspermia:

1) Direct panspermia - Spores were planted on Earth by intelligent alien creatures.
   a) The DNA was the form of life already existing on the alien planet.
   b) The DNA was from life created by intelligent beings on the alien planet.
2) Lithopanspermia - Spores were transferred to Earth by natural means without intelligent intervention.

Let us first look at Option 1a). The alien planet would have formed, simple life would have originated, and advanced life would have evolved to a point where they could send spores to Earth. However, there is a serious problem. Where did the DNA life system come from? It had to be a DNA-based system since that is what appeared on Earth. We have the same problem in knowing how life originated on Earth. Where is the intelligent input to provide the complex code of DNA? We have just transferred the problem to another planet without adding any value.

Option 1b) partially solves that problem, with the intelligent life on the alien planet developing the DNA

---

[7] Ward, Peter D. and Brownlee, Donald. 2004. *Rare Earth, Why Complex Life is Uncommon in the Universe*, New York, NY: Copernicus Books.

system and providing the initial code for simple life. But then, you must ask: Where did the intelligent life that created the DNA system on the alien planet come from? So, we are right back where we started. Furthermore, there is significant additional time for the transfer to occur. Advanced life would have had to evolve, and the DNA-coding system would have had to be developed along with the transport system.

Option 1) has an additional problem. Why would aliens send life to Earth? If this is an experiment, then, you would expect feedback, and that would entail either alien travel to Earth, or some sort of sample retrieval to be sent back to the alien planet. Either way, that would mean another trip to Earth and back. Maybe that is why we keep seeing flying saucers? Are they checking on progress of their life experiment? However, from the time life was originally planted on Earth until now is 3.5 billion years. That is a long time to see the results of an experiment unless you are a transcendental being like God. Given all of these facts, I believe we can dismiss Option 1 because of the long times and the fundamental problem of the information code in the DNA.

Option 2) has the shortest time for life transfer. The alien planet would have formed, and primitive life would have originated. Then, as soon as primitive life formed on the alien planet, there could have been an event that launched spores into space that traveled to Earth. Option 2) has the same problem of: Where did the existing DNA life form come from? How did it originate on the alien planet? Is not this the same problem again with the origin-of-life on Earth?

The scientists who support the panspermia hypothesis think they have solved the origin-of-life on Earth question, when in effect all the hypothesis does is to transfer the fundamental problem from Earth to some other planet and does nothing to provide an answer. If we know how life formed on an alien planet, then we should know how it formed on Earth. I see no discussion of how life originated on these alien planets.

Finally, the Cambrian Explosion is a strong argument against panspermia. How does panspermia explain the sudden appearance of the new life forms?

It looks like panspermia is the adult version of the Tooth Fairy. In summary, the most reasonable answer to the origin-of-life question is that God created life, an action that you would expect a theistic God to do.

Conclusion

You now know how life began on Earth. Forget about biopoiesis, endosymbiosis, spontaneous generation, clay theory, catastrophism, molecular evolution, organic evolution, panspermia, and all other theories you run across.[8] They are all wrong. **The secular truth is that the origin-of-life was a supernatural event, brought about by the Intelligent Designer, God, just as the Bible says**.

---

[8] http://www.smashinglists.com/top-10-theories-on-beginning-of-life-on-Earth/2/. [Accessed 9 June 2015]. I am not going to cover each of these theories, but you can look them up if interested.

INDEX